TEASHOP
TREATS

Shopping
List

- ✓ Butter
- ✓ Flour
- ✓ Eggs
- ✓ Sugar

TEASHOP TREATS

Create your favourite British baking classics at home

Published by The Reader's Digest Association, Inc.
London • New York • Sydney • Montreal

NOTES ON THE RECIPES
Eggs are free-range and medium, unless
stated otherwise.

Butter is unsalted.

1 tsp = 5ml; 1 tbsp = 15ml.
A teaspoon or tablespoon is level, unless
otherwise stated.

For fan ovens you may need to reduce
the temperature by up to 20°C and
reduce cooking time by 5 minutes, but
every oven is different so check before
the end of the cooking time. Resist
opening the oven during the early
stages of baking a cake, as it may
prevent it rising.

Contents

Introduction 6

Cakes 9

Buns and teacakes 39

Small cakes and slices 57

Biscuits 79

Savouries 95

Pies and tarts 111

Index 124

Introduction

Busy lives mean that a visit to a teashop or hotel for afternoon tea is, for most of us, an occasional treat. Now you can recreate the teashop experience in your own home with this selection of classic recipes. Afternoon tea is a sophisticated alternative to lunch and dinner, and is a perfect way to celebrate a special occasion, or just to get together with old friends. It is also an easy choice for entertaining at home, as you can prepare almost everything in advance; when your guests arrive you only need to make the tea and pour it. Plan to make a lovely cake or a batch of scones once in a while, and invite a few friends round – they will love you for it!

SETTING THE SCENE
Afternoon tea is traditionally served in a sitting room, so you don't need a large house or even a dining room to entertain a few guests. Somewhere to set out the plates, tea cups and teapot is essential, but this could be on a tray, or on a coffee or side table. A tablecloth over your table is practical as well as attractive, and large cotton napkins are useful for keeping clothes and fingers clean. Get out your nicest plates, cups and saucers, and a cake stand; vintage and mismatched looks great, so hunt around for some pretty gems. You will also need a china teapot and milk jug.

Put on some music; piano or dance tunes from the 1930s will set the scene. Fresh flowers look and smell lovely: choose something seasonal or picked from the garden, such as a small pot of lavender or freshly cut roses. Have as much ready as possible before guests arrive so that you don't have to keep going backwards and forwards to the kitchen, other than for more hot tea.

PLANNING YOUR MENU
To give you an idea of what to serve if planning your own afternoon tea at home, traditional afternoon tea served in a hotel

or teashop would follow the order below, but don't feel you need
to serve all of these: 1 Savouries and sandwiches; 2 Scones; 3 Cakes
and pastries.

SAVOURIES AND SANDWICHES
Make sandwiches that are easy to eat in one or two bites, so they
are not too filling. Neat rectangles or triangles with the crusts cut
off are traditional. The Ritz in London serves smoked salmon,
cucumber, egg mayonnaise, roast ham and Cheddar cheese.
Choose bread to complement the fillings, such as wholemeal
or rye with salmon, or a tomato bread with egg mayonnaise. In
the winter, slices of quiche or individual pastry tartlets would be
lovely, especially if served warm. Small slices of toasted rarebit are
very easy to make and taste delicious.

SCONES
Warm, freshly baked scones are a traditional part of afternoon tea.
Plain scones or lightly fruited with juicy sultanas or apple are best
served with butter or with small bowls of good jam and thick or
clotted cream, so your guests can help themselves.Warm cheese
scones with butter are a tasty savoury option.

CAKES AND PASTRIES
Even those who tend not to eat cake can often be tempted by
something homemade. A cake you have baked yourself with
good quality ingredients is always worth the calories. At home,
there is no need to provide the range of cakes and pastries you
might have in a teashop or hotel – one or two homemade cakes
will be very much appreciated. Choose two contrasting recipes,
such as a light sponge cake, and perhaps one rich fruit cake or
something unusual. Guests are more likely to take a small piece

of something, so individual cakes or tartlets are welcome. If your afternoon tea is for a special occasion, such as a birthday, replace the individual cakes with one special cake that can be cut and shared. When serving a choice of cakes, choose a range of textures and flavours, such as a fruit cake, something chocolatey, and something light, such as lemon. This should mean that there is something everyone will enjoy, and guests may be able to manage a small slice of each!

TEA AND OTHER DRINKS

A generous pot of hot black tea such as Darjeeling, Earl Grey or Lady Grey is perfect for afternoon tea with friends. Purists insist on loose leaves, as the larger, fresher leaves impart more flavour, and of course the pot should be warmed first and the water must be boiling. You will need a tea strainer to catch any stray leaves when you pour. Provide jugs of cold milk, slices of lemon and sugar cubes. Prepare the tea when your guests are settled, as it will taste stewed if left too long. On a hot day, large jugs of iced tea are a lovely alternative. Chilled Champagne, jugs of elderflower cordial or fresh lemonade make a gorgeous start to a special occasion tea. Coffee is traditionally served in the morning, but you may like to have some ready in case a guest prefers it to tea.

SENDING OUT INVITATIONS

Whether your tea party is for a special occasion or is simply a way to get friends together, consider sending out invitations. A few details such as the time you plan to start and finish will help guests to plan their day. You may even like to suggest a dress code, such as vintage tea dresses for the ladies and blazers or tweeds for the men. Handwritten invitations are rarely sent now, so to receive one is a treat in itself and sets the tone for your tea party.

Cakes

Dundee cake

This Scottish rich fruit cake, made with dried fruit, ground almonds and sherry, keeps very well. The traditional circular topping of blanched almonds adds crunch.

375g plain flour
1 tsp baking powder
250g soft butter, plus extra for greasing
285g caster sugar
4 eggs, lightly beaten
80ml sweet sherry or milk
225g currants
185g sultanas
180g glacé cherries

3 tbsp mixed peel, chopped
80g ground almonds
grated zest of 1 orange and 1 lemon
155g whole blanched almonds

Serves: 12
Preparation time: 20 minutes
Cooking time: 2¼–2½ hours

1 Grease a 20cm round cake tin with butter and line it with baking parchment. Preheat the oven to 160°C (gas mark 3).

2 Sift the flour and baking powder into a bowl. Cream the butter and sugar together until light and creamy. Beat in the eggs and the flour mixture, a little at a time, beating well after each addition. Stir in the sherry or milk to mix to a soft, dropping consistency. Fold in the fruit, peel, ground almonds and grated zest.

3 Spoon the mixture into the prepared tin and smooth the top. Arrange the almonds in concentric circles on top of the cake, and press them lightly into place.

4 Bake in the centre of the oven for 1 hour, then cover the top with a sheet of foil to prevent the almonds overbrowning. Cook for a further 1¼–1½ hours or until firm to the touch; a skewer inserted into the centre should come out clean. Remove from the oven and leave in the tin to cool completely before turning out.

5 Keep for 2–3 days in an airtight container before serving to allow the cake to mature and the flavours to develop.

Anglesey cake

A light sponge fruit cake, with a touch of mixed spice, this cake originates from the Isle of Anglesey, Wales. Treacle is added to give a little extra richness.

100g margarine, plus extra for greasing
75g soft brown sugar
1 egg
1 tbsp black treacle
275g self-raising flour
¼ teaspoon salt
1 tsp ground ginger
1 tsp ground mixed spice

½ teaspoon bicarbonate of soda
200ml milk
175g mixed raisins and currants

Serves: 12
Preparation time: 20 minutes
Cooking time: 50–60 minutes

1 Grease a 20cm round cake tin with margarine and line it with baking parchment. Preheat the oven to 180°C (gas mark 4). Cream the margarine and sugar together until light and creamy. Beat in the egg and mix in the black treacle.

2 Sieve together the flour, salt, ground ginger and mixed spice and stir them into the creamed mixture.

3 Dissolve the bicarbonate of soda in the milk and add gradually to the mixture. Stir in the dried fruit. Spoon the mixture into the prepared tin and bake in the preheated oven for 50–60 minutes. When cool, turn out from the tin. The cake is best kept for 24 hours before cutting.

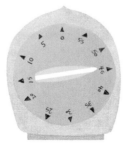

Rich fruit ring cake

Packed with delicious dried fruits including dates, cranberries and pears, and decorated with cherries and nuts, this is a good choice for a special occasion. Make 2–3 weeks before you want to eat it.

85g dried cranberries
85g sultanas
85g dried pears
85g stoned prunes
85g dried figs
85g stoned dried dates
250ml apple juice
55g pecan nuts, chopped
55g preserved ginger, chopped
grated zest and juice of 1 lemon
5 tbsp sunflower oil, plus extra for greasing
1 egg
80g dark brown sugar
125g self-raising flour
115g self-raising wholemeal flour

1 tsp baking powder
2 tsp ground mixed spice
3–4 tbsp milk

For decoration:
2 tbsp apricot jam
55g glacé cherries
30g hazelnuts
35g pecan nut halves
35g walnut halves
55g preserved ginger, sliced
icing sugar, to dust

Serves: 18
Preparation time: 40 minutes, plus soaking
Cooking time: 1¼–1½ hours

1 Grease a 23cm ring cake tin with a little sunflower oil. Preheat the oven to 150°C (gas mark 2). Chop all the dried fruits into small pieces and place in a saucepan with the apple juice; bring slowly to the boil over a moderate heat. Simmer gently, covered, for about 4 minutes or until the fruit begins to absorb the liquid.

2 Remove the pan from the heat and leave, covered, until completely cold. Stir in the pecan nuts, ginger, lemon zest and juice.

3 Beat the sunflower oil, egg and brown sugar together.

4 Sift the flours, baking powder and mixed spice into a large bowl, tipping in any bran left in the sieve. Add the soaked fruit and the

egg mixture, and stir well to combine. Stir in enough of the milk to make a fairly soft mixture.

5 Spoon the mixture into the prepared tin and smooth the top. Bake for 1¼–1½ hours or until risen, firm and golden brown; the cake should be beginning to shrink away from the side of the tin.

6 Leave the cake to cool in the tin for at least 1 hour before running a knife around the edge and turning it out. Wrap the cake in baking paper and foil and store for 2–3 weeks before serving, to allow the flavours to mature.

7 To decorate the cake, heat the apricot jam with 1 teaspoon of water over a low heat. Brush the top of the cake with the jam. Gently press the cherries, nuts and ginger into the jam to make attractive circles. Dust with sifted icing sugar before serving.

Boiled fruit cake

Perfect for celebrations as well as an afternoon treat, this rich, moist cake will keep well for several months. You can cover it with marzipan and icing for a special occasion, or eat it as it is.

900g mixed dried fruit
320g dates, chopped
100g chopped glacé cherries
125g butter, plus extra for greasing
185g soft brown sugar
2 tsp ground mixed spice
185ml sherry, plus an extra 60ml

2 eggs
80g apricot jam
150g self-raising flour
150g plain flour
50g blanched almonds

Serves: 12
Preparation time: 20 minutes
Cooking time: 2 hours

1 Put the fruit, butter, sugar, mixed spice and 185ml sherry in a large saucepan over a medium–low heat. Stir until the butter has melted and the mixture comes to the boil. Allow to boil for 3 minutes, then remove from the heat and leave to cool.

2 Meanwhile, preheat the oven to 160°C (gas mark 3). Grease a 20cm round cake tin with butter and line with a double layer of baking parchment, so that the cake won't cook too fast.

3 When the fruit mixture is cold, stir in the eggs and jam, mixing well. Sift the flours over the top and stir until well combined. Spoon the mixture into the cake tin and smooth the top. Decorate with the almonds in concentric circles.

4 Bake for 2 hours, or until a cake skewer inserted into the centre of the cake comes out clean. Pour the extra sherry on to the hot cake as soon as you remove it from the oven, so it seeps into the cake.

5 Wrap the cake in a thick tea towel and leave to cool. When cold, remove the towel, turn out the cake, and wrap the cake in greaseproof paper or foil. Store in an airtight container until you want to serve it.

Seed cake

Delicious, crunchy caraway seeds work well with the rich buttery texture of this cake. Seed cake has been popular since the 18th century when it was eaten to celebrate seed planting.

sunflower oil, for greasing
175g soft butter
175g golden caster sugar
1 tbsp caraway seeds
2 large eggs, separated
175g self-raising flour

pinch of salt
55g ground almonds

Serves: 8
Preparation time: 20 minutes
Cooking time: 50 minutes

1 Preheat the oven to 180°C (gas mark 4). Grease a 900g loaf tin with sunflower oil and line it with baking parchment.

2 Put the butter and sugar in a bowl and beat together until light and creamy. Add the caraway seeds and stir well to mix. Beat in the egg yolks, one at a time. Sift the flour, then fold into the mixture with the salt and ground almonds.

3 In a clean bowl, whisk the egg whites until stiff. Fold them into the cake mixture, a little at a time.

4 Spoon the mixture into the prepared tin and bake for about 50 minutes or until a skewer inserted into the middle of the cake comes out clean.

5 Transfer the tin to a wire rack and leave to cool for about 10 minutes before turning the cake out on to the rack to cool completely. Slice when cold and serve on its own or with low-fat crème fraîche and strawberries.

Cold tea cake

Soaking sultanas, currants and dates in tea adds juiciness and a lovely flavour. And of course this cake is delicious with a hot cup of tea! This is a very easy cake to make; simply measure out the ingredients using a tea cup.

1 cup cold tea
125g margarine, plus extra for greasing
1 cup mixed sultanas and currants
1 cup dates, chopped
1 cup brown sugar

2 cups self-raising flour
1 tsp mixed spice
1 tsp bicarbonate of soda

Serves: 6
Preparation time: 15 minutes
Cooking time: 1 hour

1 Put the tea, margarine, fruit and sugar in a large saucepan over a low heat and bring to the boil, stirring from time to time. Simmer for 3 minutes, then remove from the heat and set aside until cool.

2 Preheat the oven to 180°C (gas mark 4). Grease a 20cm round cake tin with margarine and line it with baking parchment. Sift the flour, spice and bicarbonate of soda together then stir into the cooled tea mixture, mixing thoroughly.

3 Spoon the mixture into the prepared tin and bake in the pre-heated oven for about 1 hour or until a skewer inserted into the centre of the cake comes out clean.

4 Transfer the tin to a wire rack and leave to cool for about 10 minutes before turning the cake out to cool completely.

Genoese sponge cake

Whisking together the eggs and sugar makes this a really light sponge cake, and is the usual method for gâteaux in France. Use the very best jam and cream you can find for this classic cake.

4 eggs
110g caster sugar, plus extra for sprinkling
½ tsp vanilla extract
100g plain flour
60g butter, melted, plus extra for greasing

For the filling:
115g strawberry jam
325ml double or whipping cream

Serves: 8
Preparation time: 25 minutes
Cooking time: 20 minutes

1 Grease two 20 cm straight-sided sandwich tins and line the bases with baking parchment. Preheat the oven to 190°C (gas mark 5).

2 Beat or whisk the eggs and sugar in a large heatproof bowl over a saucepan of simmering water until thick and creamy. Sift the flour into the bowl and, using a metal spoon, carefully fold it into the creamed mixture. Gently fold in the cooled melted butter and vanilla extract.

3 Spoon the mixture equally between the two tins and spread evenly. Bake for 20 minutes or until the cakes are well risen, springy to the touch and have shrunk slightly from the sides of the tins. Leave to cool for 10 minutes, then turn out on to a wire rack and leave to cool completely.

4 Place one cake upside-down on a serving plate and spread evenly with the jam. Whisk the cream until it is thick enough to hold its shape and spread evenly over the jam, just up to the edge of the sponge. Place the second cake on top of the filling and sift the extra caster sugar evenly over the top.

Grandma's never-fail sponge

We've used lemon curd to fill this traditional sponge sandwich cake, but fruit jam would be lovely too. For a chocolate version, add 2 tablespoons of cocoa powder to the flour, and fill with buttercream.

melted butter, for brushing
110g self-raising flour
50g cornflour
4 eggs, at room temperature
170g caster sugar
1 tsp vanilla extract
sifted icing sugar, for dusting

For the filling:
4 tbsp lemon curd
4 tbsp whipped cream

Serves: 8
Preparation time: 20 minutes
Cooking time: 20 minutes

1 Preheat the oven to 180°C (gas mark 4). Grease two shallow 20cm round cake tins with melted butter and line the bases with baking parchment.

2 Sift the flour and cornflour three times. Using an electric mixer, beat the eggs, sugar and vanilla in a bowl for 8 to 10 minutes, or until light and creamy.

3 Gently fold in the flour mixture, then spoon the mixture into the cake tins and bake for 20 minutes, or until the cakes are golden and beginning to shrink away from the sides of the tins.

4 Remove the cakes from the oven and leave in the tins for 10 minutes, then turn out on to a wire rack to cool.

5 When the cakes are cold, place one sponge on a serving plate. Spread generously with the lemon curd and cream. Place the remaining sponge cake on top and dust with icing sugar.

Basic butter cake

A very easy but light and fluffy cake that tastes of vanilla and butter. A delicate orange butter icing works well as a topping for this cake, or you could try using lemon zest and juice instead.

200g butter, softened
170g caster sugar
2 tsp vanilla extract
3 eggs, lightly beaten
185g self-raising flour
110g plain flour
125ml milk

For the icing:
155g icing sugar
grated zest of 1 orange
1½ tbsp butter, softened
1 tbsp orange juice or milk,
  as needed

Serves: 8
Preparation time: 15 minutes
Cooking time: 45 minutes

1 Preheat the oven to 180°C (gas mark 4). Grease a deep 20cm round cake tin and line it with baking parchment.

2 Beat the butter, sugar and vanilla in a bowl until light and creamy. Add the beaten eggs gradually, beating well after each addition. Sift the flours together. Fold the flour and the milk alternately into the butter mixture.

3 Spoon the cake mixture into the cake tin and smooth the surface. Bake for 45 minutes. Remove the cake from the oven and leave in the tin for 10 minutes before turning out on to a wire rack to cool completely.

4 To make the icing, sift the icing sugar into a bowl. Add the orange zest and butter and mix gently. Gradually add enough orange juice or milk so that the mixture forms a thick but spread-able consistency. Spread the icing over the top.

Victoria sandwich

Named after Queen Victoria, this sponge cake was served at tea
parties at her home Osborne House on the Isle of Wight. The
classic afternoon tea cake, do try to bake it at least once.

125g soft butter, plus extra
for greasing
125g caster sugar
2 eggs
125g self-raising flour, sifted
1 tsp vanilla extract
icing sugar, for dusting

For the filling:
4 tbsp raspberry jam

Serves: 8
Preparation time: 15 minutes
Cooking time: 20–25 minutes

1 Preheat the oven to 190°C (gas mark 5). Grease two 15cm
sandwich tins and line the bases with baking parchment. Cream
together the butter and sugar until light and creamy.

2 Beat in the eggs, one at a time, adding one teaspoon of the flour
before adding the second egg.

3 Fold in the rest of the flour and the vanilla extract. Spoon
the mixture evenly between the two prepared tins. Bake in the
preheated oven for 20–25 minutes until the cakes are well risen
and springy to touch. Turn out and leave to cool on a wire rack.

4 Sandwich the cakes together with the raspberry jam. Dust the
top of the cake with icing sugar.

Madeira cake

This classic English buttery cake was served with Madeira wine in the 18th century, particularly when guests came to visit, and it has kept the name. Madeira cake is equally delicious with a cup of tea.

225g self-raising flour
¼ tsp salt
175g soft butter, plus extra for greasing
175g caster sugar
4 eggs
2 strips of citron peel

Serves: 8
Preparation time: 20 minutes
Cooking time: 1½–1 ¾ hours

1 Preheat the oven to 160°C (gas mark 3). Grease an 18 cm round cake tin and line the base and sides with baking parchment. Sieve the flour and salt together.

2 Cream the butter and sugar until light and creamy. Beat in the eggs, one at a time, adding one tablespoon of the flour mixture with each egg. Fold in the rest of the flour thoroughly and spoon the mixture into the prepared tin.

3 Bake in the preheated oven for about 30 minutes, then place the two strips of citron peel on top of the cake. Bake for a further 30 minutes, then reduce the oven temperature to 150°C (gas mark 2). Bake for a further 30–45 minutes.

4 Leave to cool in the tin for 10 minutes, then turn out the cake on to a wire rack and leave to cool completely.

Coffee walnut cake

Rich and very moreish, this variation on a sponge sandwich cake is a British teatime favourite. The coffee-flavoured icing contrasts well with the crunchy walnuts.

100g margarine, plus extra for greasing
100g caster sugar
2 large eggs
50g walnuts, chopped
1 tbsp coffee essence
100g self-raising flour
1 tsp baking powder

For the filling and topping:
75g butter
225g icing sugar
2 tsp milk
2 tsp coffee essence
walnut halves, for decoration

Serves: 8
Preparation time: 20 minutes
Cooking time: 35–40 minutes

1 Preheat the oven to 160°C (gas mark 3). Grease two 18cm sandwich tins and line the bases with baking parchment.

2 Put the margarine and sugar, eggs, walnuts and coffee essence in a bowl. Add the self-raising flour and baking powder. Mix until the ingredients are well combined.

3 Divide the mixture between the prepared tins, level the surfaces and bake in the preheated oven for 35–40 minutes, or until well risen and springy to the touch.

4 Turn the cakes out on a wire rack to cool.

5 Meanwhile make the filling: beat the butter, icing sugar, milk and coffee essence in a bowl until smooth. Sandwich the cakes together with two-thirds of the filling, then spread the remaining filling over the top. Mark the surface with a fork in a decorative pattern. Place the walnut halves on the cake to decorate.

Banana cake

This cut-and-come-again cake is best made with very ripe bananas, so it's a good way of using up bananas that have been sitting in the fruit bowl for too long.

2 large, ripe bananas
250g self-raising flour
1 tsp baking powder
50g light muscovado sugar
6 tbsp sunflower oil, plus extra
for greasing
6 tbsp milk

2 eggs
115g sultanas

Serves: 8
Preparation time: 10 minutes
Cooking time: 50–55 minutes

1 Preheat the oven to 180°C (gas mark 4). Grease an 18cm round deep cake tin and line with baking parchment. Peel the bananas, then mash with a fork.

2 Sift the flour and baking powder into a bowl and stir in the sugar. Whisk together the oil, milk and eggs and add to the flour mixture. Stir in the sultanas and mashed bananas, then spoon the mixture into the prepared tin.

3 Bake for 50–55 minutes or until the cake is well risen and a skewer inserted into the centre comes out clean. Leave to cool for 10 minutes, then loosen the edge of the cake with a knife and turn it out on to a wire rack to cool completely.

Carrot and Brazil nut cake

A delicious carrot cake, packed with juicy raisins and crunchy Brazil nuts for extra flavour and texture. It is lovely on its own, but the light ricotta cheese frosting adds a delicious creaminess.

175g self-raising wholemeal flour
175g self-raising flour
1 tsp ground cinnamon
100g Brazil nuts
60g raisins
140g light brown sugar
200ml sunflower oil, plus extra for greasing
4 large eggs
200g carrots (about 3 carrots), finely grated

grated zest and juice of ½ orange

For the icing:
250g ricotta cheese
55g sugar, sifted
grated zest of ½ orange

Serves: 12
Preparation time: 30 minutes, plus cooling time
Cooking time: 50 minutes

1 Grease a 20cm round deep cake tin and line with baking parchment. Preheat the oven to 180°C (gas mark 4).

2 Sift the flours and cinnamon into a large bowl, tipping in any bran left in the sieve. Coarsely chop about two-thirds of the Brazil nuts and stir into flour with the raisins. Slice the remaining nuts lengthways thinly and set aside.

3 In another bowl, beat together the sugar and oil until well combined. Beat in the eggs one at a time. Stir in the grated carrots and orange zest and juice. Fold the carrot mixture into the flour mixture until combined, but do not overmix.

4 Spoon the mixture into the prepared tin and bake for 50 minutes or until risen and firm to the touch. Leave the cake in the tin for 10 minutes, then turn out on to a wire rack. Peel off the baking paper and leave to cool.

5 To make the icing, beat together the ricotta cheese, sugar and orange zest in a bowl. Spread the icing on top of cooled cake and decorate with the reserved sliced nuts, placing them so that they stick up at different angles. Store this cake, covered, in the fridge.

Cherry and almond cake

Fat, juicy glacé cherries are the feature of this classic cake. The ground almonds add a lovely crumbly texture that contrasts well with the juicy cherries.

125g margarine, plus extra for greasing
125g butter
225g caster sugar
3 eggs
¼ teaspoon almond essence
125g glacé cherries, rinsed and halved
225g plain flour

125g ground almonds
1 level tsp baking powder
¼ tsp salt
1 tbsp granulated sugar

Serves: 8
Preparation time: 25 minutes
Cooking time: 1½–2 hours

1 Preheat the oven to 160°C (gas mark 3). Grease a 20cm cake tin and line with a double layer of baking parchment. Cream together the margarine, butter and caster sugar until light and creamy.

2 Beat the eggs and almond essence together and mix into the creamed mixture. Stir in the glacé cherries.

3 Sieve the flour, ground almonds, baking powder and salt together and fold in. Spoon the mixture into the tin and smooth the top.

4 Sprinkle the cake with the granulated sugar and bake in the preheated oven for 1½–2 hours.

5 Allow the cake to cool in the tin for 10 minutes, then turn out on to a wire rack and leave to cool completely.

Date and walnut loaf

Dark and caramel-rich with brown sugar, dates and walnuts, this
moreish loaf is wonderful served warm from the oven or left to
cool and spread with a little butter a day or two later.

160g dates, chopped
185g soft brown sugar
3 tbsp butter, plus extra for
greasing
½ tsp bicarbonate
of soda
1 egg, beaten

60g walnuts, chopped
300g self-raising flour

Serves: 6–8
Preparation time: 20 minutes
Cooking time: 45–50 minutes

1 Preheat the oven to 180°C (gas mark 4). Grease a 2lb loaf tin,
and line it with baking parchment.

2 Combine the dates, sugar, butter and 250ml water in a saucepan
over a medium–low heat and stir until the sugar has dissolved.
Bring to the boil briefly, then remove from the heat and set aside
to cool until the mixture is lukewarm.

3 Add the bicarbonate of soda, egg and walnuts and mix well.
Sift the flour over the mixture and stir until well combined.
Spoon the mixture into the loaf tin.

4 Place the tin on a baking tray and bake for 45–50 minutes or
until a skewer inserted into the middle of the loaf comes out
clean. Allow the loaf to cool in the tin for 10 minutes, then turn
out on to a wire rack to cool.

Hazelnut meringue cake

Simply add sparklers or long wand candles to turn this light but gooey meringue into a birthday cake. It has a light pastry cream and fresh raspberry filling.

65g hazelnuts
4 egg whites
225g caster sugar

To decorate:
225g fresh raspberries
sifted icing sugar, to decorate

For the cream:
300ml milk, plus 2 tbsp extra
if needed

1 vanilla pod, slit open
lengthways
3 egg yolks
30g caster sugar
15g plain flour
15g cornflour

Serves: 6
Preparation time: 40 minutes,
plus 30 minutes standing
Cooking time: 1¼ hours

1 Preheat the grill, then toast the hazelnuts until golden. Leave to cool. Roughly chop a few for the decoration and set aside, then finely chop or grind the rest of the hazelnuts in a nut mill or food processor.

2 Preheat the oven to 140°C (gas mark 1). Line two baking sheets with baking parchment and draw a 20cm diameter circle on each piece of parchment.

3 Whisk the egg whites in a large bowl until they form stiff peaks. Gradually whisk in the caster sugar a tablespoon at a time, then continue to whisk for 1–2 minutes or until the meringue is very thick and glossy. Fold in the finely chopped or ground hazelnuts with a large metal spoon.

4 Divide the meringue between the baking sheets and spread evenly within the drawn circles. Bake for 1¼ hours or until the meringues are set. Loosen the meringues from the paper, then leave to cool completely on the baking sheets.

5 To make the vanilla pastry cream, pour the milk into a saucepan and bring to the boil. Add the vanilla pod, then remove from the heat and leave the milk to infuse for 30 minutes.

6 Whisk the egg yolks with the caster sugar for 2–3 minutes or until pale. Sift in the flour and cornflour, and whisk to combine.

7 Remove the vanilla pod from the milk and scrape the seeds into the milk with a sharp knife; discard the pod. Bring the milk to the boil, then remove from the heat and whisk it gradually into the egg and flour mixture.

8 Pour the mixture back into the saucepan and bring to the boil, stirring constantly with a wooden spoon or a whisk. When thick, simmer gently for 1 minute, still stirring constantly. Remove from the heat. Cover the surface of the pastry cream with wet greaseproof paper and leave to cool.

9 Assemble the cake just before serving. Place one of the meringues on a serving plate, flat side uppermost, and spread over the pastry cream (if it is too thick to spread, beat in the extra milk). Sprinkle with two-thirds of the raspberries, then top with the second meringue. Decorate with the remaining raspberries, roughly chopped toasted hazelnuts and a dusting of icing sugar.

Spanish orange and almond cake

Made with whole oranges – simmered until very tender and then finely chopped – and ground almonds, this classic Spanish cake has a moist, light texture and a wonderful fresh flavour.

2 large oranges, scrubbed and roughly chopped (with skin)
butter, for greasing
5 eggs, separated
200g caster sugar
225g ground almonds

2 tbsp flaked almonds
sifted icing sugar, for dusting

Serves: 10
Preparation time: 1 hour
Cooking time: 50–55 minutes

1 Put the chopped oranges in a small saucepan, discarding any pips. Add one tablespoon of water, then cover and cook gently for 30 minutes or until the oranges are soft and any liquid has evaporated. Set aside to cool.

2 Preheat the oven to 180°C (gas mark 4). Grease a 23cm springform round cake tin with butter and line with baking parchment. Finely chop the oranges in a food processor or with a large knife.

3 Put the egg whites in a large bowl and whisk until they form stiff peaks. Gradually whisk in half the caster sugar, then whisk for 1 minute.

4 Whisk the egg yolks with the remaining caster sugar in a separate bowl for 2–3 minutes or until pale and quite thick. Whisk in the finely chopped oranges, then carefully fold in the ground almonds.

5 Stir in 3 spoonfuls of the whisked egg white to loosen the mixture, then gently fold in the remaining whites using a large metal spoon. Transfer the mixture to the prepared tin and level the top. Sprinkle with the flaked almonds.

6 Bake for 50–55 minutes or until the cake is golden and a skewer inserted in the centre comes out clean. Check the cake after 30 minutes, and cover lightly with foil if it is browning too quickly.

7 Leave the cake to cool in the tin, then turn it out, peel away the lining paper and transfer to a serving plate. Dust with icing sugar before serving.

Honey cake

Soured cream and honey give a wonderful moistness to this buttery cake. A scattering of toasted flaked almonds adds a nutty richness and cuts through the sweetness a little.

250g soft butter, plus extra for greasing
195g soft brown sugar
1 tsp vanilla extract
175g honey
3 eggs
225g self-raising flour
75g plain flour
1 tsp ground cinnamon
250ml soured cream

For the topping:
20g butter
260g honey
90g flaked almonds, toasted

Serves 10
Preparation time: 20 minutes
Cooking time: 1 hour

1 Preheat the oven to 160°C (gas mark 3). Grease a 22cm round springform cake tin with butter and line it with baking parchment.

2 Cream together the butter, sugar and vanilla in a bowl until light and creamy. Add the honey and mix until combined. Add the eggs, one at a time, beating well after each addition.

3 Sift the flours and cinnamon over the top and gently stir in with the soured cream until combined. Spoon the mixture into the tin, smooth the surface and bake for 1 hour or until a skewer inserted into the middle of the cake comes out clean. Remove the cake from the oven and leave in the tin for 10 minutes, then turn out on to a wire rack to cool.

4 To make the topping, melt the butter and honey in a small saucepan over a medium heat. Stir until the mixture comes to the boil, reduce the heat and simmer for 2 minutes. Remove from the heat and stir in the almonds.

5 When the cake has cooled, spread the topping over the top and sides of the cake.

Somerset apple cake

If you have a glut of apples, use them in this delicious cake. You will find variations of this in all apple-growing areas. Add a tablespoon of Someset apple cider or brandy for extra flavour.

sunflower oil, for greasing
175g soft butter
175g light muscovado sugar
3 eggs, beaten
1 tbsp black treacle
225g wholemeal self-raising flour
100g self-raising flour
¼ tsp ground nutmeg
½ tsp ground cinnamon
¼ tsp ground ginger
675g cooking apples, peeled and chopped
3 tbsp skimmed milk

Serves: 8
Preparation time: 20 minutes
Cooking time: 1¼ hours

1 Preheat the oven to 160°C (gas mark 3). Grease a 24cm round cake tin with sunflower oil and line it with baking parchment. Cream the butter and sugar together until light and creamy, then beat in the eggs a little at a time. Add the treacle and stir until well combined.

2 Sift in the flours and spices, stir to mix, then add the apple. Add enough of the milk to make a soft batter and mix lightly.

3 Spoon the mixture into the tin, level the top and bake for about 1¼ hours or until a skewer inserted into the middle of the cake comes out clean.

4 Leave to cool in the tin for at least 10 minutes, then turn the cake out on to a wire rack to cool. Serve warm on its own or with a little crème fraîche.

Strawberry shortcake

This streamlined version of an American classic is based on a
quick, light scone mixture and is filled with yogurt, whipped
cream and lots of juicy fresh strawberries... simply irresistible!

250g self-raising flour, plus
extra for dusting
1 tsp baking powder
90g butter, diced, plus extra
for greasing
3 tbsp caster sugar
1 egg, beaten
80ml milk
½ tsp vanilla extract

For the filling and decoration:
350g strawberries
90ml cream, for whipping
90g natural yogurt
1 tsp icing sugar

Serves: 8
Preparation time: 15 minutes
Cooking time: 10–15 minutes

1 Preheat the oven to 220°C (gas mark 7). Sift the flour and
baking powder into a bowl and rub in the butter until the mixture
resembles fine breadcrumbs. Stir in the sugar.

2 Combine the egg, milk and vanilla extract and pour into a well
in the centre of the dry ingredients. Combine the ingredients and
then draw them together with your hands into a soft dough. Pat
into a smooth ball and place on a floured work surface.

3 Roll out the dough into a 19cm round. Place on a greased baking
tray then bake in the preheated oven for 10–15 minutes or until
well risen, firm and browned on the top. Slide the shortcake on to
a wire rack and leave to cool.

4 Using a large serrated knife, slice the shortcake horizontally in
half. Cut the top layer into eight equal wedges. Trim a fraction off
each so that there is a little space between them when you place
them on top of the shortcake. Place the remaining slice on a
serving plate.

5 Set aside eight strawberries then hull and slice the remainder.
Whip the cream until soft peaks form, then stir in the yogurt.

6 Spread the cream mixture thickly over the bottom shortcake layer and cover with the sliced strawberries, pressing them into the cream.

7 Place the shortcake wedges on top of the fruit, then sift over the icing sugar. Slice the reserved strawberries lengthwise, leaving the slices attached at the stalk end. Fan them out slightly and place one on each shortcake wedge.

Rich chocolate cake with fudge icing

The thick chocolate fudge icing makes this a very rich cake, ideal for birthdays and special occasions. Use the best dark chocolate you can find. This cake dates back to the 17th century.

225g plain flour
2 level tsp baking powder
½ level tsp bicarbonate of soda
¼ tsp salt
50g plain chocolate
225ml milk
150g soft butter, plus extra for greasing
275g dark, soft brown sugar
3 eggs
1 tbsp black treacle
1 tsp vanilla extract

For the icing:
450g granulated sugar
150ml milk
125g butter
1 level tbsp golden syrup
1 heaped tbsp cocoa powder
50g plain chocolate

Serves: 8
Preparation time: 50 minutes
Cooking time: 30–35 minutes

1 Preheat the oven to 180°C (gas mark 4). Grease three 18cm sandwich tins and line the bases with baking parchment. Sift together the flour, baking powder, bicarbonate of soda and salt.

2 Put the chocolate with the milk in a small saucepan over a low heat and stir until the chocolate has melted. Remove the pan from the heat and allow the mixture to cool.

3 Cream the butter and sugar together until light and creamy. Beat in the eggs, one at a time, adding a little of the flour mixture alternately with each egg. Stir in the treacle and vanilla extract and fold in the remaining flour. Mix well, then gradually stir in the cooled chocolate and milk to make a thick batter.

4 Spoon the mixture between the three tins and bake in the

preheated over for 30–35 minutes. Turn out the cakes on to a cake rack and leave to cool.

5 To make the icing, put the sugar, milk, butter, golden syrup, cocoa powder and chocolate in a large, heavy-based pan. Heat gently and stir until the sugar has dissolved, then bring to the boil and cook until fudgy. To test, drop a little of the mixture into a bowl of cold water, leave for 1 minute and then squeeze between forefinger and thumb; it should form a soft ball which can be squashed slightly. Leave to cool for 10 minutes, then beat until it is thick enough to spread.

6 Sandwich the cake layers together with the icing. Spread the remaining icing over the top and sides of the cake, swirling it with a knife. It sets fairly rapidly, so work quickly.

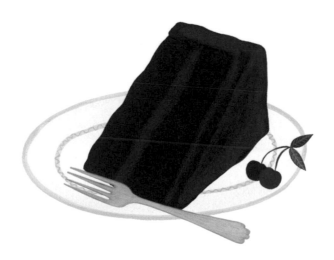

Rich chocolate torte

A generous amount of good-quality dark chocolate makes this Continental-style cake beautifully moist and rich – just a small slice will satisfy any sweet tooth. It's perfect with a cup of tea.

170g dark chocolate (at least 70% cocoa solids)
75g butter, plus extra for greasing
4 eggs
100g light muscovado sugar
30g plain flour

Serves: 10
Preparation time: 20 minutes
Cooking time: 15–20 minutes

1 Preheat the oven to 180°C (gas mark 4). Grease a 23cm round cake tin with butter and line it with baking parchment.

2 Break up the chocolate and put it in a heatproof bowl with the butter. Set the bowl over a pan of almost boiling water, making sure the water is not touching the base of the bowl. Stir until melted, then remove from the heat.

3 Meanwhile, put the eggs and sugar in a large bowl and beat with an electric mixer until the mixture has increased considerably in volume and leaves a trail on the surface when the beaters are lifted out. (If using a hand whisk or rotary beater, set the bowl over a pan of almost boiling water while you whisk, making sure the water is not touching the base of the bowl.)

4 Add the chocolate mixture to the whisked mixture and fold it in with a metal spoon. Sift the flour over the top and fold in until it is combined.

5 Spoon the mixture into the prepared cake tin, gently spreading it to the edges, and level the surface. Bake for 15–20 minutes or until the top of the cake feels just firm to the touch. Leave to cool in the tin before turning out.

Buns
and teacakes

· ·

Big fruity tea bun

A big, fat loaf bun that you cut into thick wedges to share with friends. Serve when it is still warm from the oven. Shop-bought buns never taste or smell as good as this!

3 tsp dried yeast
4 tsp caster sugar
300g plain flour, plus extra for dusting
2 tbsp butter, diced, plus extra melted butter, for brushing
1 egg, lightly beaten
125g sultanas

For the glaze:
1 tbsp caster sugar
1 tbsp powdered gelatine

For the icing:
60g icing sugar
1 tbsp milk
2 tsp butter
a few drops of pink food colouring
1 tbsp desiccated coconut

Serves: 6
Preparation: 20 minutes, plus 40 minutes rising
Cooking: 20–25 minutes

1 Combine the yeast, 1 teaspoon sugar and 185ml warm water in a jug. Stand in a warm place for 5–10 minutes, or until frothy.

2 Sift the flour into a large bowl. Rub in the butter using your fingertips until the mixture resembles fine breadcrumbs, then stir in the remaining sugar. Mix the yeast mixture, egg and sultanas into the flour mixture until the dough comes together. Cover with clingfilm and rest in a warm place for 30 minutes, or until the dough has doubled in size.

3 Meanwhile, preheat the oven to 200°C (gas mark 6). Brush a baking tray with a little melted butter.

4 Turn the dough out on to a lightly floured surface and knead for 5–8 minutes, or until smooth. Knead into a 20cm round shape, place on the baking tray and leave to rest for 10 minutes, or until well risen.

5 Bake for 20–25 minutes, or until the bun is golden and sounds hollow when tapped on the base. Transfer to a wire rack.

6 To make the glaze, combine the sugar, gelatine and 1 tablespoon of hot water in a saucepan and heat until the gelatine and sugar have dissolved. Brush the glaze over the bun and allow to cool.

7 To make the icing, sift the icing sugar into a bowl. In a small saucepan heat the milk and butter until the butter has melted. Add to the icing sugar and stir until smooth, then add the food colouring, one drop at a time, until a pale pink colour is reached.

8 Spread the icing over the cooled bun and sprinkle with the desiccated coconut.

Blackcurrant fruit loaf

Tart blackcurrants make an excellent summer cake that is fruity without being too sweet. Mint adds a fresh herbal note. This loaf will keep well in the freezer for up to two months.

340g self-raising flour
45g butter, diced, plus extra for greasing
115g brown sugar
125g fresh blackcurrants
3 tbsp chopped fresh mint

125ml orange juice, or as needed

Serves: 8
Preparation time: 20 minutes
Cooking time: 1¼ hours

1 Preheat the oven to 180°C (gas mark 4). Sift the flour into a large bowl and rub in the butter using your fingertips until the mixture resembles fine breadcrumbs. Stir in the sugar and make a well in the centre.

2 Place the blackcurrants and mint in the well and pour in the orange juice. Stir the ingredients until thoroughly combined; the mixture should be soft. Add a little more orange juice if necessary.

3 Grease a 30 x 11cm loaf tin with butter and line it with baking parchment. Spoon the mixture into the prepared tin and smooth the top. Bake for about 1¼ hours or until cake has risen and is firm to the touch. Check the loaf after about 50 minutes; if it is browning too much, loosely place a piece of foil over the top.

4 Leave the cake to cool in the tin for 5 minutes, then turn it out on to a wire rack to cool completely. For the best flavour, leave overnight before serving.

Cinnamon raisin bread

This milk-enriched raisin bread tastes good plain or can be served spread with a little honey or jam. It's also wonderful the day after baking, toasted and spread with butter.

450g strong wholemeal flour
1½ tsp salt
2 tsp ground cinnamon
3 tsp dried yeast
115g raisins
45g caster sugar
55g butter, plus extra for greasing

240ml milk, plus 1 tbsp to glaze
1 egg, lightly beaten

Serves: 8
Preparation time: 20 minutes, plus 1 hour rising
Cooking time: 30 minutes

1 Sift the flour, salt and cinnamon into a large mixing bowl, tipping in any bran left in the sieve. Stir in the yeast, raisins and sugar, and make a well in the centre.

2 Heat the butter and milk in a small saucepan until the butter has melted. Pour into the dry ingredients and add the beaten egg. Mix together to make a soft dough.

3 Turn the dough out on to a lightly floured surface and knead for 10 minutes or until smooth and elastic. Grease a 900g loaf tin with butter and line with baking parchment. Shape the dough and place in the prepared tin. Cover with oiled clingfilm or a clean tea towel and leave to rise in a warm place for about 1 hour or until doubled in size.

4 Towards the end of the rising time, preheat the oven to 220°C (gas mark 7). Uncover the loaf and brush with the milk to glaze. Bake for about 30 minutes or until it sounds hollow when tapped. Check the loaf after 25 minutes, and if it looks as if it is browning too much, loosely place a piece of foil over the top.

5 Turn out on to a wire rack and leave to cool.

Malted sultana bread

Malt extract adds a delicious sweet richness to fruit breads. You can find it in healthfood shops. This sultana bread keeps well. Serve it sliced thickly and spread with butter and jam.

200g strong wholemeal flour, preferably stoneground
150g strong white flour
½ tsp salt
1 tsp dried yeast
3 tbsp malt extract
1 tbsp clear honey
200ml tepid water

85g sultanas
sunflower oil, for greasing

Serves: 6
Preparation time: 20 minutes, plus 2 hours rising
Cooking time: 35–40 minutes

1 Sift the wholemeal and white flours and the salt into a large bowl, tipping in any bran left in the sieve. Add the yeast and stir well to mix.

2 Stir the malt extract and honey into the tepid water, and pour into a well in the flour. Gradually work the flour into the liquids to make a soft but not sticky dough. Knead in the sultanas.

3 Turn the dough out on to a lightly floured surface and knead for about 10 minutes or until very elastic. Place the dough in a greased bowl, cover with clingfilm and leave to rise in a warm place for about 1 hour or until doubled in size. Meanwhile, grease a 450g loaf tin with sunflower oil and line with baking parchment.

4 Turn the dough out on to the floured work surface again then knock the dough back by punching it with your knuckles. Gently shape the dough and put it into the prepared tin. Cover with a damp tea towel and leave to rise in a warm place for 1 hour until doubled in size.

5 Preheat the oven to 190°C (gas mark 5). Uncover the loaf and bake for 35–40 minutes or until it sounds hollow when tapped. Turn it out on to a wire rack and leave to cool.

Bara brith

Still made widely in Wales, Bara brith ("speckled cake") has been a family favourite for generations. Some versions do not use yeast and are more like fruit loaf cakes. This version is lovely toasted.

275g strong white flour
1 level tsp salt
20g lard
25g sugar
1 level teaspoon ground mixed spice
1 large egg, beaten
150ml warm water
20g fresh yeast

225g currants
125g sultanas
25g chopped mixed diced peel

Serving: 6
Preparation time: 20 minutes, plus 1 hour rising
Cooking time: 35 minutes

1 Sieve the flour and salt into a large mixing bowl. Rub in the lard using your fingertips until it resembles fine breadcrumbs, then make a well in the centre. Mix the sugar and spice together and put into the well.

2 Combine the beaten egg with the warm water and use 3 tablespoons of it to mix the yeast to a smooth, thin paste, then stir in the rest of the liquid. Pour over the sugar then mix well. Knead well to make a smooth, elastic dough.

3 Mix together the currants, sultanas and peel and knead lightly into the dough.

4 Mould the dough into a round or long shape, as you prefer, and put on a greased baking sheet or into a greased 900g loaf tin. Cover with greased clingfilm and put in a warm place to rise for 1 hour. Meanwhile, preheat the oven to 180°C (gas mark 4). Bake in the oven for 35 minutes. Turn it out on to a wire rack and serve warm or leave to cool.

Barm brack

This fruit-packed Irish loaf is similar to both Bara brith from Wales and Selkirk bannock from the Scottish Borders. It is traditionally served at Hallowe'en, when rings or coins are wrapped up and hidden inside the dough before it is baked.

450g strong white flour
¼ tsp grated nutmeg
½ tsp ground mixed spice
pinch of salt
55g golden caster sugar
3 tsp dried yeast
25g butter, diced, plus extra for greasing
about 250ml tepid milk

225g mixed currants and sultanas
55g chopped mixed peel
1 tbsp golden granulated sugar

Serves: 8
Preparation time: 20 minutes, plus 3 hours rising
Cooking time: 40 minutes

1 Sift the flour, spices and salt into a bowl. Stir in the caster sugar and yeast, then rub in the butter using your fingertips until the mixture resembles fine breadcrumbs. Make a well in the centre, then add enough tepid milk to form a soft dough, adding more liquid if needed.

2 Turn the dough out on to a floured board and knead for about 10 minutes until smooth. Knead in the dried fruit and peel, a handful at a time.

3 Place in a lightly greased bowl, cover with greased clingfilm and put in a warm place for 2 hours, or until well risen.

4 Grease an 18cm deep round cake tin with butter. Knock back the dough by punching it with your knuckles, then shape the dough into the tin. Cover loosely and leave in a warm place for another hour or so, or until the dough has risen nearly to the top of the tin.

5 Meanwhile, heat the oven to 220°C (gas mark 7).

6 Bake for 15 minutes, then reduce the heat to 190°C (gas mark 5) and continue to cook for about 20 minutes until the base sounds hollow when tapped.

7 Meanwhile, bring 1 tablespoon of water to the boil in a small saucepan, add the granulated sugar and dissolve over a low heat. Once the barm brack is done, remove from the oven, brush the top with the glaze and return it to the oven for 3 minutes.

8 Turn out on to a wire rack to cool. Serve warm, sliced, as it is or lightly spread with butter.

Treacle gingerbread loaf

Thick dark treacle, rich brown sugar and a generous measure of
mixed spice and golden ground ginger – there's a lot to enjoy
about this spicy loaf which will stay moist for days if properly
wrapped and stored.

butter, for greasing	260g black treacle
185g plain flour	185ml milk
110g self-raising flour	80ml olive oil
1 tsp bicarbonate of soda	2 eggs
1 tbsp ground ginger	**Serves:** 8
3 tsp ground mixed spice	**Preparation:** 20 minutes
140g soft brown sugar	**Cooking:** 40–45 minutes

1 Preheat the oven to 180°C (gas mark 4). Grease a 450g loaf tin
with butter and line with baking parchment, ensuring that the
paper extends 3cm above the tin.

2 Sift the flours, bicarbonate of soda, ginger and mixed spice into
a large bowl. Stir in the sugar until well combined. Whisk the
treacle, milk, olive oil and eggs in a jug. Add to the flour mixture
and stir until combined.

3 Spoon the mixture into the loaf tin and bake for 40–45 minutes,
or until a skewer inserted into the middle comes out clean.
Remove from the oven and leave in the tin for 10 minutes, then
turn out on to a wire rack and allow it to cool completely.

Spiced oatmeal parkin

The north of England has some wonderful recipes for parkin, an oatmeal-based rich gingerbread. Not only can it be made in advance, it also improves with keeping.

sunflower oil, for greasing
175g self-raising flour
175g medium oatmeal
pinch of salt
85g butter, diced
1 tsp ground ginger
¼ tsp ground nutmeg
85g light muscovado sugar

2 tbsp black treacle
1 egg
150ml buttermilk

Serves: 8
Preparation time: 20 minutes
Cooking time: 60–70 minutes

1 Heat the oven to 160°C (gas mark 3). Grease a 900g loaf tin with sunflower oil and line it with baking parchment. Put the flour, oatmeal and salt in a bowl and stir to mix. Rub in the butter using your fingertips until the mixture resembles breadcrumbs, then stir in the ginger, nutmeg and sugar.

2 Warm the treacle in a small saucepan until just melted, then beat in the egg. Pour the warmed treacle and egg mixture into the dry ingredients, add the buttermilk and stir well.

3 Spoon the mixture into the tin and bake for 60–70 minutes, until a skewer inserted into the middle comes out clean.

4 Remove the tin to a wire rack and leave to cool in the tin before turning out. When completely cold, cut into squares to serve.

Bath buns

Those who live in the city from which this bun takes its name claim that the genuine article can be bought only there, and call those made elsewhere the 'London Bath Bun'.

1 large egg, beaten
150ml warm water
2 tsp caster sugar
20g fresh yeast
325g strong white flour, plus extra for dusting
25g granulated sugar
75g soft butter, plus extra for greasing
125g sultanas
125g roughly crushed lump sugar
25g chopped candied lemon peel

grated zest of 1 lemon
a little beaten egg, to glaze
roughly crushed lump sugar, for sprinkling

Makes: 16
Preparation time: 45 minutes
Fermenting, rising and resting time: 2¼ hours
Cooking time: 10 minutes.

1 Stir the beaten egg and warm water together. Dissolve the caster sugar in it and use 3 tablespoons of this liquid to mix the yeast to a smooth paste. Stir in the remaining liquid and whisk in 50g of the flour to make a smooth batter. Cover the bowl with clingfilm and put in a warm place to rise for 30 minutes.

2 To make the dough, sieve the remaining flour into a large mixing bowl and make a well in the centre. Add the granulated sugar and pour in the egg and yeast mixture. Mix until the sugar has dissolved, then gradually draw in the flour and work the ingredients together to form a stiff dough.

3 Knead in the softened butter a little at a time until the dough has a silky look. Shape it into a ball, then wrap it in greased clingfilm and leave in a warm place for 1 hour, or until the dough has nearly trebled in size.

4 Preheat the oven to 230°C (gas mark 8). Turn the dough on to a floured surface and put the sultanas, crushed lump sugar, candied peel and lemon zest on top. Knead them in until they are evenly distributed and the dough has a smooth texture. Cover it with clingfilm and leave for 5 minutes.

5 Divide the dough into 16 pieces by pulling and tearing, not cutting. Put the rough pieces, well spaced out, on a lightly buttered, warmed baking sheet, cover with clingfilm and leave to rise in a warm place for 15–20 minutes.

6 Brush the buns over lightly with beaten egg, sprinkle a little crushed lump sugar on top and leave to rise, uncovered, for 20 minutes. Bake in the preheated oven for about 10 minutes, or until golden brown.

Teacakes

These lightly spiced teacakes are simple to make and delicious served split, lightly toasted and spread with a little butter or jam. These are best eaten on the day, but can be kept for 1–2 days.

225g strong white flour, plus extra for dusting
225g strong wholemeal flour
1 tsp salt
55g butter, diced
3 tsp dried yeast
30g caster sugar
85g sultanas
85g currants
½ tsp ground cinnamon
300ml tepid milk, plus extra for brushing

Makes: 10
Preparation time: 25 minutes, plus 3 hours rising
Cooking time: 10–15 minutes

1 Sift the flours and the salt into a large bowl, tipping in any bran left in the sieve. Rub in the butter using your fingertips, then stir in the yeast, sugar, sultanas, currants and cinnamon. Make a well in the centre and pour in the milk. Mix together, adding more milk as needed to make a soft dough.

2 Turn the dough out on to a lightly floured surface and knead for about 10 minutes or until smooth and elastic. Place in a lightly greased bowl, cover with a tea towel and leave to rise in a warm place for 1–2 hours until doubled in size.

3 Turn the dough out on to the lightly floured surface and knock out any air bubbles. Knead for 2–3 minutes, then divide it into 10 equal pieces. Shape each piece into a round teacake. Place the teacakes on two greased baking sheets and cover with a damp tea towel. Leave to rise in a warm place for 1 hour until puffy.

4 Meanwhile preheat the oven to 220°C (gas mark 7). Uncover the teacakes and lightly brush the tops with milk. Bake for 10–15 minutes until nicely browned, then transfer to a wire rack to cool.

Cinnamon teacake

A sprinkling of sugar and cinnamon is all it takes to turn a simple teacake into something special. If you really love cinnamon, you can add a pinch to the batter before you bake it.

80g soft butter, plus extra for greasing
145g caster sugar
1 tsp vanilla extract
1 egg
200g self-raising flour
200ml milk

For the topping:
1 tablespoon melted butter
1 tablespoon caster sugar, mixed with ½ teaspoon ground cinnamon

Serves: 6
Preparation: 10 minutes
Cooking: 35 minutes

1 Preheat the oven to 180°C (gas mark 4). Grease a 20cm round cake tin with butter and line it with baking parchment.

2 Using an electric mixer, beat the butter, sugar and vanilla extract in a bowl until the mixture is almost white. Add the egg and beat until well combined. Sift the flour, then fold the flour and milk into the batter until combined. Spoon the mixture into the cake tin and smooth the surface.

3 Bake for 30–35 minutes or until a skewer inserted into the middle comes out clean. Remove from the oven and leave in the tin for 10 minutes to cool slightly, then turn out on to a wire rack.

4 While the cake is still warm, brush the top with the melted butter and sprinkle with the sugar mixture. Serve warm or cold.

Chelsea buns

In the late 17th and early 18th centuries, all fashionable London came to the Chelsea Bun House in the Pimlico Road to eat the delicious buns, spicy, rich with fruit and hot from the oven.

For the ferment and dough:
1 large egg, beaten
215ml warm water
25g fresh yeast
525g strong white flour
90g sugar
¼ teaspoon salt
50g soft butter, plus extra for brushing
granulated sugar, for sprinkling
ground mixed spice or ground cinnamon, for sprinkling
25–50g sultanas
caster sugar, for topping

Makes: 12
Preparation time: 45 minutes
Fermenting, resting and rising time: 1 hour and 55 minutes
Cooking time: 12 minutes

1 To make the ferment, mix together the beaten egg and warm water. Mix the yeast to a smooth paste with 3 tablespoons of the liquid. Add the remaining liquid and whisk in 125g of the flour and 15g of the sugar to make a smooth batter. Cover with a damp tea towel and put in a warm place to ferment for 30 minutes.

2 To make the dough, sieve the remaining flour and salt into a large mixing bowl and make a well in the centre. Add the remaining sugar and pour the ferment over it. Stir until the sugar has dissolved, then gradually draw in the flour and mix well to make a soft dough.

3 Knead in the softened butter thoroughly until the dough looks smooth and silky. Shape it into a ball, put it in a greased bowl, cover with greased clingfilm and leave in a warm place to rise for 45 minutes.

4 Turn out the risen dough on to a working surface and knock out any air bubbles using your knuckles. Roll out the dough to

a rectangle about 23 x 30cm. Brush the dough with the melted butter, leaving a 1.5 cm strip uncoated along one shorter edge. Brush this strip with water.

5 Sprinkle granulated sugar thinly over the butter, then dust lightly with mixed spice or cinnamon. Scatter the sultanas over the dough and roll it up from the buttered shorter edge, stretching it slightly while rolling so that the sugar and fruit is gripped tightly. Seal the roll by pressing the moistened edge down firmly.

6 Brush the roll all over with more melted butter, then cut into slices 2 cm thick, to give 12 pieces. Lay the pieces 1.5cm apart on a greased baking sheet, setting them cut side up. Cover with greased clingfilm and leave to rise in a warm place for 40 minutes. Preheat the oven to 220°C (gas mark 7).

7 Bake in the preheated oven for 12 minutes. As the buns rise and are baked, they will spread together and become square. Once they are baked, sprinkle immediately with the caster sugar. Separate the buns when they are nearly cold.

Kentish huffkins

Soft, oval-shaped bread rolls with a characteristic dent in the middle – often filled with jam – huffkins were baked throughout Kent, especially at the end of the hop-picking season.

3 tsp dried yeast
1 tsp sugar
450g strong white bread flour
1 tsp salt
40g butter, diced, plus extra for greasing
225ml tepid mixture of milk and water

Makes: 12
Preparation time: 15 minutes, plus 2 hours rising
Cooking time: 15 minutes

1 Put the yeast, sugar, flour and salt in a large bowl, then rub in the butter using your fingertips until the mixture resembles fine breadcrumbs. Make a well in the centre and add the milk and water gradually, working it into the dry ingredients to make a stiff dough. Turn the dough on to a floured surface and knead for up to 10 minutes until smooth and elastic.

2 Place the dough in a lightly greased bowl. Cover with a damp tea towel and leave in a warm place for 1–1½ hours, until well risen.

3 Knock back the risen dough by punching it with your knuckles, then divide the mixture into 12 pieces. Shape each into an oval and place on a greased baking sheet. Make a small dent in the middle of each oval with your fingertip. Loosely cover again and leave to rise in a warm place for 30–40 minutes. Meanwhile, heat the oven to 220°C (gas mark 7).

4 Bake for 15 minutes or until the huffkins sound hollow when tapped on the base. Remove to a wire rack to cool.

Small cakes
and slices

Scones

Afternoon tea served in a hotel or teashop will always include
freshly baked plain or fruit scones.

450g self-raising flour, plus
extra for dusting
80g butter, diced, plus extra
for greasing
250ml milk, plus extra, for
brushing

To serve:
strawberry jam
clotted or whipped cream

Makes: 12
Preparation: 10 minutes
Cooking: 20 minutes

1 Preheat the oven to 200°C (gas mark 6). Grease and lightly flour
a baking tray.

2 Sift the flour into a large bowl. Using your fingertips, rub in the
butter until the mixture resembles fine breadcrumbs. Make a well
in the centre. Stir in the milk until it forms a dough, adding a little
more milk if the dough is too dry.

3 Turn the dough out on to a lightly floured surface and lightly
knead – don't overmix or the scones will be tough.

4 Gently press the dough out into a round shape about 2cm thick.
Using a 5cm round cutter, cut out 12 scones. Place on the baking
tray, 1cm apart. Brush with a little milk and
bake for 20 minutes or until lightly
golden and well risen. Transfer
to a wire rack to cool slightly.
Serve warm, with spoonfuls
of jam and cream.

Blackberry and lemon scones

Make these scones when firm, sweet blackberries are in season.
The addition of buttermilk to the mixture ensures the result is
light and flaky.

125g self-raising flour
115g self-raising
wholemeal flour
1 tsp baking powder
55g caster sugar
55g butter, diced, plus extra
for greasing
grated zest of 1 lemon

85g fresh blackberries
125ml buttermilk, or more
as needed

Makes: 8
Preparation time: 15 minutes
Cooking time: 20–25 minutes

1 Grease a baking tray. Preheat the oven to 200°C (gas mark 6).
Sift the flours and baking powder into a large bowl, tipping in any
bran left in the sieve. Stir in the sugar. Rub in the butter using
your fingertips until the mixture resembles fine breadcrumbs.

2 Stir in the lemon zest, and then very gently stir in the
blackberries, taking care not to overmix as the blackberries can
easily become crushed.

3 Lightly stir in the buttermilk and, again, be careful not to crush
the fruit. Add a little more buttermilk if there are any dry bits of
dough remaining in the bowl.

4 As soon as the mixture comes together in a soft dough, lift it on
to a lightly floured work surface and knead gently two or three
times only, just enough to form a rough ball.

5 Pat out the dough carefully with your hands to make an 18cm
round shape. Transfer to the baking tray, and gently mark the top
into eight wedges. Sprinkle with a little extra white flour. Bake for
20–25 minutes or until risen and lightly golden. Serve warm,
broken into the marked wedges.

Chocolate éclairs

For real wow-factor, try making these classic French cream-filled choux buns. They are not difficult to make, but your guests will never know. Use good-quality chocolate for the topping.

For the pastry:
50g butter, plus extra for greasing
150ml water
65g plain flour
pinch of salt
2 eggs, beaten

For the filling and icing:
300ml double cream
1 tbsp caster sugar
100g plain chocolate

Makes: 12–14
Preparation time: 40 minutes
Cooking time: 35–40 minutes

1 Preheat the oven to 220°C (gas mark 7). To make the pastry, put the butter and water in a heavy-based pan and cook over a low heat until the butter melts, then raise the heat and rapidly bring the mixture to the boil.

2 Take the pan off the heat and sift in the flour and salt. Stir quickly with a wooden spoon until the flour has been absorbed by the liquid and comes away from the sides of the pan.

3 Leave the pastry to cool slightly, then beat in the eggs, a little at a time, beating well after each addition. Continue beating until the paste is shiny. The paste should be thick enough to hold its shape, but not too stiff to pipe.

4 Spoon the choux pastry into a piping bag fitted with a 1cm plain nozzle. Grease a baking tray, then pipe out 7.5cm lengths on to the tray.

5 Bake the éclairs in the preheated oven for 15 minutes, then reduce the temperature to 190°C (gas mark 5) and continue baking for 20–25 minutes until crisp. Slit the éclairs down one side and leave on a wire rack to cool.

6 To make the filling, whip the double cream with the sugar, then spoon it into a piping bag fitted with a plain nozzle. Fill the cold éclairs with the cream.

7 Break the chocolate into squares and place them in a heatproof bowl. Stand the bowl over a pan of hot water, stirring occasionally, until the chocolate melts. Coat the tops of the éclairs with the melted chocolate and leave to cool and set.

Blueberry muffins

Muffins are so simple to bake, and homemade ones are far more delicious than the ones you can buy. If you have any muffins left over after tea, these freeze well, and are delicious for breakfast.

260g self-raising flour
115g caster sugar
125g butter, melted
2 eggs
185ml buttermilk
1 tsp vanilla extract
150g fresh or frozen
blueberries, chopped

Makes: 12
Preparation: 10 minutes
Cooking: 15–20 minutes

1 Preheat the oven to 180°C (gas mark 4). Line a 12-hole muffin tin (with 80ml holes) with large paper muffin cases.

2 Sift the flour into a large mixing bowl. Stir in the sugar until well combined. In a large jug, whisk together the butter, eggs, buttermilk and vanilla extract. Add to the flour mixture with the berries and stir until just combined – don't overbeat or the muffins will be tough.

3 Spoon the mixture into the paper cases. Bake for 15–20 minutes, or until a skewer inserted into the centre of a muffin comes out clean. Lift the muffins out of the tray on to a wire rack and leave to cool.

Chocolate muffins

Freshly baked chocolate muffins smell wonderful, and taste terrific with a cup of tea. This recipe uses good chocolate and a dash of brandy so the muffins are not too sweet, and will appeal to adults.

125g plain chocolate (with at least 70% cocoa solids), broken into pieces
75g butter, diced
3 eggs
60g icing sugar, sifted
2 tbsp ground almonds
1 tbsp plain flour, sifted
1 tbsp brandy (optional)

Makes: 8
Preparation: 10 minutes
Cooking: 8 minutes

1 Preheat the oven to 240°C (gas 9). Line a muffin tray with eight paper muffin cases.

2 Melt the chocolate in a heatproof bowl over a saucepan of simmering water (or melt gently in the microwave). Stir well, then remove the bowl from the heat and stir in the butter – it will melt in the warmth of the chocolate.

3 Break the eggs into a separate clean bowl and whisk them for 3–4 minutes until thick and foamy. Stir in the sifted icing sugar, ground almonds and flour. Now fold in the melted chocolate mixture and the brandy, if using.

4 Divide the mixture among the paper muffin cases. Bake for 8 minutes or until well risen and firm to the touch. Lift the muffins out of the tray on to a wire rack and leave to cool.

Chocolate brownies

Almost no one can resist these dark, moist, fudgy, chocolatey treats. Bake a batch and watch them vanish. Or if you can bear to, wait a day or two and enjoy them in their chewy perfection.

butter, for greasing
250g butter, chopped
200g dark chocolate, roughly chopped
325g soft brown sugar
4 eggs, lightly beaten
1 tsp vanilla extract

185g plain flour, sifted
100g dark chocolate chips
sifted icing sugar, for dusting

Makes: 12
Preparation: 20 minutes
Cooking: 35 minutes

1 Preheat the oven to 160°C (gas mark 3). Grease a 28 x 18cm baking tin and line with baking parchment.

2 Melt the butter and the 200g chopped chocolate in a saucepan over a low heat. Whisk in the sugar until the sugar melts, then set aside for 5 minutes to cool.

3 Whisk in the eggs and vanilla extract, then stir in the flour. Add the chocolate chips and stir to combine.

4 Spoon the mixture into the baking tin. Bake for 35 minutes, or until the top is firm and the cake is coming away from the sides of the tin – it should still be very moist inside.

5 Remove from the oven and allow to cool completely in the tin. Cut into 12 pieces and serve dusted with icing sugar.

Chocolate coconut squares

These cakes are popular all over Australia, where they are named Lamingtons after a former Governor of Queensland. Use any sponge cake you like – the point here is the delicious coating.

250g icing sugar
40g cocoa powder
60ml milk
180g desiccated coconut
2 x 20 cm square sponge cakes
100g raspberry jam

Makes: 16
Preparation: 20 minutes
Cooking: none required

1 To make the icing, sift the icing sugar and cocoa powder into a bowl. Add the milk and 60ml boiling water and stir until smooth.

2 Spread the coconut on a plate. Place one of the sponge cakes on a flat surface. Spread with the jam, then top with the other sponge cake. Cut the sandwich cake into 16 small squares.

3 Using two forks, roll a square of cake in the chocolate icing until well coated, allowing any excess to drip off. Drop the cake into the coconut and roll with your fingers to coat well. Transfer to a wire rack to set. Coat the remaining cake squares in the same way.

Jam and coconut slice

A layer of raspberry jam is baked inside these delicious soft slices. The coconut adds a lovely nutty flavour and texture that works well with the jam and sponge. A teatime or cake stall favourite.

3 tbsp soft butter, plus extra for greasing
170g caster sugar
225g self-raising flour
2 eggs
315g raspberry jam

For the topping:
2 eggs
115g caster sugar
135g desiccated coconut

Makes: 24
Preparation: 15 minutes
Cooking: 30 minutes

1 Preheat the oven to 180°C (gas mark 4). Grease a shallow 20 x 30cm baking tin and line it with baking parchment.

2 Combine the butter, sugar and flour in a food processor and pulse until the mixture resembles fine breadcrumbs. Add the eggs and pulse until a dough forms. If necessary, add a little water to bring the mixture together.

3 Press the mixture into the baking tin and spread the jam evenly over the top.

4 To make the topping, beat the eggs and sugar in a large bowl until pale and creamy, using an electric mixer. Add the coconut and stir through. Pour the topping over the jam, spreading to cover it evenly.

5 Bake for 30 minutes or until golden and firm. Remove from the oven and leave to cool in the tin. Cut into 24 slices to serve.

Chocolate peppermint slice

Rich, sophisticated flavours and colours make this a perfect treat at any time. Try going for the best grade of chocolate you can find – you'll really appreciate the difference in flavour.

250g plain chocolate-
flavoured biscuits
150g butter, melted
250g icing sugar, sifted
1 tsp peppermint extract
50ml milk, as needed
200g dark chocolate,
roughly chopped
1 tbsp vegetable oil

Makes: 24
Preparation: 20 minutes,
plus 10 minutes setting
Cooking: 2–3 minutes

1 Line a shallow 20 x 30cm baking tin with baking parchment.

2 Put the biscuits in a food processor and blend until finely chopped. Combine the biscuit crumbs and melted butter and press evenly into the tin. Place the tin in the freezer while preparing the topping – this will make the biscuit base harden, so that it will be easier to spread the topping over it.

3 In a bowl, mix together the icing sugar, peppermint extract and milk – the mixture should be of a spreading consistency, so add a little more milk if necessary. Spread the icing over the hardened biscuit base and return to the freezer.

4 Place the chocolate in a heatproof bowl over a saucepan of simmering water, ensuring the base of the bowl doesn't touch the water. Stir the chocolate for 2–3 minutes until melted, then stir in the vegetable oil.

5 Spread the chocolate mixture over the slice and set aside for about 10 minutes to harden. To serve, cut into 24 squares using a hot knife. Store in the fridge for up to three days.

Chocolate cherry slice

Another tempting slice with a really rich and chewy filling of coconut and cherries. And it's so easy to make – you don't even need to bake it.

250g plain digestive biscuits
150g butter, melted

For the filling:
397g can sweetened condensed milk
250g desiccated coconut
400g glacé cherries, finely chopped
100g white vegetable shortening such as Cookeen, melted

For the topping:
200g dark chocolate, roughly chopped
1 tablespoon white vegetable shortening

Makes: 24
Preparation: 20 minutes, plus up to 1 hour setting
Cooking: 2–3 minutes

1 Line a shallow 20 x 30cm baking tin with baking parchment.

2 Put the biscuits in a food processor and blend until finely chopped. Combine the biscuit crumbs and melted butter and press evenly into the baking tin. Place the tin in the freezer while preparing the topping – this will make the biscuit base harden, so it will be easier to spread the topping over it.

3 Combine all the filling ingredients in a large bowl and mix well. Press the filling evenly over the biscuit base, using wet hands to smooth the surface.

4 To make the topping, melt the chocolate and shortening in a heatproof bowl for 2–3 minutes over a saucepan of simmering water, ensuring the base of the bowl doesn't touch the water. Stir well, then pour the mixture over the slice and spread evenly.

5 Set aside for up to 1 hour to harden. Cut into 24 squares using a hot knife. Store in the fridge for up to three days.

Lemon slice

Topped with a baked sweet and tangy custard, these slices are very moreish. Lemon slices would be good served alongside a slice of fruit cake and chocolate cake for a special afternoon tea.

200g soft butter	125ml lemon juice
60g icing sugar	75g plain flour
225g plain flour	sifted icing sugar, for dusting

For the topping:	**Makes:** 24
6 eggs	**Preparation:** 15 minutes
345g caster sugar	**Cooking:** 40 minutes
grated zest of 1 lemon	

1 Preheat the oven to 180°C (gas mark 4). Line a 20 x 30cm baking tin with baking parchment.

2 Combine the butter, icing sugar and flour in a food processor and process until it comes together in a ball – it may be necessary to add a teaspoon of cold water to bring the mixture together.

3 Press the dough evenly into the baking tin and prick several times with a fork. Bake for 25 minutes, or until lightly golden.

4 Meanwhile, make the topping. Place the eggs in a bowl and whisk. Mix in the sugar, lemon zest and lemon juice. Sift the flour over the mixture and whisk to combine.

5 Pour the mixture over the biscuit base and bake for a further 15 minutes, or until the topping has just set. Remove from the oven and leave to cool in the tin. Cut into 24 squares and dust with icing sugar.

Just-right rock cakes

Rock cakes are so simple and ideal for encouraging children to try baking. Children can help to stir in the currants and mixed peel and everyone will enjoy the results. Ideal with a cup of tea.

300g self-raising flour
½ tsp baking powder
½ tsp ground cinnamon
80g butter, chopped
80g caster sugar, plus extra for sprinkling
150g currants

2 tbsp mixed peel
125ml milk
1 egg

Makes: 20
Preparation: 10 minutes
Cooking: 15–20 minutes

1 Preheat the oven to 200°C (gas mark 6). Line two baking trays with baking parchment.

2 Sift the flour, baking powder and cinnamon into a large bowl. Using your fingertips, rub in the butter until it resembles fine breadcrumbs. Stir in the sugar, currants and mixed peel.

3 Whisk the milk and egg together in a jug, then add to the flour mixture and stir through – the mixture should be quite stiff.

4 Spoon heaped tablespoons of the mixture on to the baking trays, about 5cm apart, to allow room for spreading. Sprinkle with a little extra sugar and bake for 15–20 minutes, or until golden and cooked through. Remove from the oven and leave to cool on the baking trays.

Iced fairy cakes

Fairy cakes are easy to prepare and always popular with children so would be a good choice for a birthday tea or when friends come round. These are topped with pretty crystallised violets.

125g soft butter
125g caster sugar
2 eggs
100g self-raising white flour
30g self-raising wholemeal flour
½ tsp baking powder
grated zest of 1 orange

For the icing:
250 g ricotta cheese
55 g icing sugar
grated zest of 1 orange
crystallised violets to decorate

Makes: 18
Preparation: 20 minutes
Cooking time: 20 minutes

1 Preheat the oven to 180°C (gas mark 4). Line a 12-cup and a 6-cup shallow bun tin with small paper cake cases.

2 Put the butter, sugar and eggs in a large bowl. Sift the white and wholemeal flours and the baking powder into the bowl, tipping in any bran left in the sieve. Add the orange zest and beat with an electric mixer for 2 minutes or until light and creamy.

3 Spoon the mixture into the paper cake cases. Bake for about 20 minutes or until just springy and firm to the touch. Transfer to a wire rack to cool.

4 To make the icing, put the ricotta cheese in a bowl and sift in the icing sugar. Add the orange zest and beat with a wooden spoon until well mixed.

5 Spread a little icing over the top of each cake and decorate with a piece of crystallised violet.

Chorley cakes

Similar to Eccles cakes, these Lancashire specialities are made with
a light shortcrust pastry and filled with currants and butter. Serve
them with a piece of Lancashire cheese; the combination is lovely.

225g plain flour
115g strong white flour
1 tsp baking powder
25g golden caster sugar
150g butter, diced
pinch of salt
125ml skimmed milk
sunflower oil, for greasing
1 egg, beaten, to glaze

For the filling:
225g currants
55g light muscovado sugar
25g butter, melted

Makes: 6
Preparation time: 30 minutes,
   plus 30 minutes resting
Cooking time: 30 minutes

1 Sift the flours and baking powder into a food processor. Add
the sugar, butter and salt. Process until the mixture resembles
breadcrumbs then, with the machine still running, slowly pour
in enough milk to form a fairly stiff dough. Alternatively, rub the
butter into the dry ingredients in a large bowl using your fingers,
adding milk to make a stiff dough.

2 Wrap the dough in cling film and refrigerate for 30 minutes.
Heat the oven to 190°C (gas mark 5). For the filling, mix together
the currants, sugar and melted butter.

3 Roll out the pastry to a thickness of about 5mm. Using a saucer
or small plate as a template, cut out six rounds of pastry, each
about 20cm in diameter.

4 Divide the filling between the pastry rounds and spread it
evenly. Moisten the edges of the pastry with water, then draw
the edges up together to meet in the middle and form a package,
pinching the edges together lightly to seal.

5 Turn the package upside down so that the edges are underneath.
Using a rolling pin, gently roll out each package until the currants

are just beginning to show through. They will now be about 10cm in diameter.

6 Place on a lightly greased baking sheet and brush all over with beaten egg. Make two parallel slits on top of each cake and bake for 30 minutes or until golden brown.

7 Remove to a wire rack to cool for at least 20 minutes. Serve slightly warm or cooled completely.

Flapjacks with apricots

Flapjacks contain healthy oats, and this recipe uses honey instead
of syrup, so this would make a good lunchbox treat too. Adding
mashed banana is unusual for flapjacks and adds moisture.

100g butter, plus extra
for greasing
75g light muscovado sugar
3 heaped tbsp honey
350g porridge oats
(not jumbo oats)

pinch of salt
100g dried apricots, chopped
1 banana, mashed

Makes: 24
Preparation time: 15 minutes
Cooking time: 20–25 minutes

1 Heat the oven to 180°C (gas mark 4) and lightly butter a
23 x 33cm swiss roll tin.

2 Melt the butter, sugar and honey in a saucepan, then add the
oats and salt. Stir to mix, then add the apricots and mashed
banana. Mix well. Spoon the mixture into the prepared tin, and
smooth the surface with the back of a metal spoon to compress it.

3 Bake for 20–25 minutes, or until firm and golden brown.

4 Cut into 24 squares while still warm, then leave to cool
completely in the tin.

Palmiers

These pretty curved French pastries are so simple and easy to make. Keep a packet of good ready-made puff pastry at home and you can make these whenever you feel like a treat.

flour, for dusting
225g ready-made puff pastry
25g caster sugar
butter, for greasing

Makes: 12
Preparation time: 15 minutes
Cooking time: 14 minutes

1 Preheat the oven to 220°C (gas mark 7). On a lightly floured surface, roll out the pastry to a rectangle of 30 x 25cm. Sprinkle the pastry with some of the caster sugar. Fold the long sides so that they meet in the centre. Sprinkle with the remaining caster sugar and fold the pastry in half lengthways, hiding the first folds. Press lightly and evenly with the fingertips along the pastry. Cut the pastry into 12 slices.

2 Grease a baking tray, then place the palmiers on the tray, cut-side down and well apart to give them room to spread. Open out the top of each palmier slightly and flatten the whole slice lightly with a round-bladed knife.

3 Bake the palmiers in the preheated oven for 10 minutes, then turn them over and bake for a further 4 minutes. Remove from the tray and cool on a wire rack.

Scotch pancakes

Scotch pancakes (also called drop scones) are easy and fun to make, and perfect for tea. Serve with fromage frais, honey and fresh berries for an irresistible afternoon treat.

125g self-raising flour
2 tsp caster sugar
1 egg, beaten
1 tbsp melted butter
150ml semi-skimmed milk
4 tsp sunflower oil

To serve:
100g blueberries
1 tsp clear honey
100g raspberries
200g fromage frais

Makes: about 24
Preparation time: 10 minutes
Cooking time: 15–20 minutes

1 Put the flour in a bowl and stir in the sugar. Make a well in the centre, and add the egg, melted butter and a little of the milk. Gradually stir the flour into the liquids and add the remaining milk a little at a time, to make a fairly thick, smooth batter.

2 Heat a large shallow dish in a low oven, then turn off the heat and line the dish with a tea towel (this is for keeping the cooked pancakes warm). Heat a griddle or large, heavy-based frying pan over a moderate heat and grease it with 1 teaspoon of the oil.

3 Using a dessertspoon, pour the batter on to the griddle from the pointed end (rather than the side of the spoon) to make neat, round circles. Depending on the size of the griddle, you should be able to cook four or five scones at once, but make sure you leave enough space round them so you can turn them easily. Cook for about 2 minutes or until almost set and bubbles are breaking on the surface; the scones should be golden brown underneath.

4 Using a palette knife, turn the scones over and cook for a further 1–2 minutes or until golden brown on the other side. Transfer to the prepared dish, wrap in the tea towel and keep warm while you

cook the remaining scones. Grease the griddle lightly with
1 teaspoon of oil before cooking each batch.

5 Place the blueberries in a bowl and stir in the honey. Add the
raspberries and lightly crush the fruit, leaving some berries whole.
Serve the scones warm with the honeyed berries and the fromage
frais spooned over.

Meringues

Delicate, cream-filled meringues piled high on your favourite plate make an impressive display. Make the meringues in advance, and sandwich them with the cream just before serving.

For the meringues:
4 egg whites
285g caster sugar

For the filling:
¼ teaspoon vanilla extract
1 tsp icing sugar
170ml cream, for whipping

icing sugar, for decoration

Makes: 8
Preparation time: 15 minutes
Cooking time: 2–3 hours

1 Line two large baking trays with baking parchment. Preheat the oven to 110°C (gas mark ½).

2 Using a large, dry mixing bowl, whisk the egg whites until stiff but not dry. Add the sugar, a tablespoon at a time, whisking until all of it is incorporated and the mixture is thick and glossy.

3 Using two tablespoons, form neat oval shapes of the mixture and place on the trays, 2.5cm apart. You have enough mixture for 16 spoonfuls. Bake for 2–3 hours or until lightly coloured on the outside and still slightly soft in the centre, like marshmallow. The time needed to dry the meringues will vary for different ovens.

4 Leave the oven door open, and leave the meringues to cool. This helps to prevent them cracking. When cool, remove from the oven and store in an airtight container until ready to fill.

5 To make the filling, whisk the vanilla extract and one teaspoon of icing sugar into the cream until thick but not buttery. Sandwich the meringues together with the cream. Place the meringues on a large serving dish and sift icing sugar lightly over them to serve.

Biscuits

Macaroons

These light almond-flavoured treats are now back in
fashion. The traditional edible rice paper that acts as a paper case
can be peeled off or eaten.

4 sheets of rice paper
125g ground almonds
170g caster sugar
1 tsp cornflour
2 egg whites, lightly beaten
¼ tsp vanilla extract
2 tbsp almonds, split

Makes: 24
Preparation time: 15 minutes
Cooking time: 15–20 minutes

1 Line two large baking trays with the sheets of rice paper. Preheat
the oven to 180°C (gas mark 4). Combine the almonds, sugar and
cornflour in a mixing bowl.

2 Beat the egg whites and vanilla extract until stiff, then fold into
the almond mixture.

3 Put teaspoonfuls of mixture in little mounds on the rice paper,
spacing them well apart. You could use a piping bag fitted with
a large plain nozzle and pipe the mixture on to the paper. Press
a split almond into the centre of each macaroon. Bake for 15–20
minutes, or until pale golden brown. Remove from the oven and
leave to cool on the trays.

4 Tear off the macaroons from the rice paper and tear off any
excess rice paper from around the sides of each macaroon. It is
fine to leave the paper on the base of each macaroon as the rice
paper is edible.

Coconut macaroons

Soft coconut contrasts beautifully with the meringue-like centres of these macaroons. They will last for at least a week in an airtight tin, so would make a great gift for a foodie friend.

2 egg whites
145g caster sugar
½ tsp cream of tartar
1 tsp vanilla extract
180g desiccated coconut

Makes: 24
Preparation: 15 minutes
Cooking: 35–40 minutes

1 Preheat the oven to 150°C (gas mark 2). Line two baking trays with baking parchment.

2 Using an electric mixer, beat the egg whites in a bowl until soft peaks form. Add the sugar, one tablespoon at a time, beating after each addition until well combined and dissolved. Fold in the cream of tartar, vanilla extract and coconut.

3 Spoon or pipe the mixture on to the baking trays. Bake for 35–40 minutes, or until the macaroons are dry to the touch. Open the oven door and leave the macaroons to cool in the oven.

Cinnamon star biscuits

Very popular in Germany, these pretty biscuits are ideal for a
Christmas tea party.

2 egg whites
pinch of salt
125g icing sugar, sifted
1 tsp ground cinnamon
grated zest of 1 lemon
175g ground almonds
55g caster sugar

Makes: 16
Preparation: 10 minutes, plus
1 hour resting
Cooking: 20 minutes

1 Whisk the egg whites and a pinch of salt in a heatproof bowl
until frothy. Add the icing sugar, cinnamon and lemon zest. Place
the bowl over a saucepan of simmering water and using an electric
mixer, beat until the mixture is thick and holds its shape well.
Remove the bowl from the saucepan.

2 Set aside about 80ml of the egg white mixture. Using a large
metal spoon, fold the ground almonds through the remaining
mixture to form a dough. Fold more ground almonds into the
mixture if it is too sticky, then set aside to rest for 1 hour.

3 Preheat the oven to 180°C (gas mark 4). Line two baking trays
with baking parchment.

4 Sprinkle half the caster sugar on a sheet of greaseproof paper.
Place the biscuit dough on top. Sprinkle with the remaining caster
sugar and place another sheet of greaseproof paper on top. Using a
rolling pin, gently roll out the biscuit dough until it is 5mm thick,
then remove the top sheet of greaseproof paper. Cut out 16 star
shapes and transfer to the baking trays.

5 Using a palette knife, spread the reserved egg white mixture over
the biscuits. Bake for 15–20 minutes or until just firm. Transfer to
a wire rack to cool.

Shortbread

These buttery, crumbly shortbread biscuits are perfect with a cup of tea. A box of homemade shortbread biscuits would make a lovely gift, so make some extras.

250g soft butter
90g icing sugar
1 tsp vanilla extract
300g plain flour, plus extra for dusting
60g cornflour

Makes: 24–28
Preparation: 20 minutes, plus 15 minutes resting
Cooking: 15–20 minutes

1 Using an electric mixer, beat the butter, icing sugar and vanilla extract in a bowl until light and creamy. Mix in the flour and cornflour using a wooden spoon.

2 Turn the dough out on to a lightly floured surface and gently knead until smooth. Divide the dough in half, then roll out each portion to form a disc about 2cm thick. Wrap the discs in greaseproof paper and refrigerate for 15 minutes.

3 Meanwhile, preheat the oven to 160°C (gas mark 3). Line two baking trays with baking parchment.

4 Roll the dough out between two sheets of baking parchment until about 5mm thick. Using a round, fluted 7cm pastry cutter, cut 12–14 rounds from each piece of dough.

5 Place the biscuits on the baking trays and bake for 15–20 minutes, or until firm to the touch. Remove from the oven and leave to cool on the trays for 10 minutes, then transfer to a wire rack to cool.

Jam drop biscuits

A children's favourite that adults will enjoy too; the jam turns
nicely chewy when baked. We've used raspberry jam, but apricot
or strawberry jam or lemon curd would taste delicious too.

125g soft butter
80g caster sugar
1 egg
150g self-raising flour
75g plain flour
30g cornflour
2 tbsp raspberry jam

Makes: about 28
Preparation: 15 minutes
Cooking: 12–15 minutes

1 Preheat the oven to 180°C (gas mark 4). Line two baking trays
with baking parchment.

2 Using an electric mixer, beat the butter and sugar in a bowl until
light and creamy. Add the egg and beat until well combined. Sift
the three flours over the mixture, then stir in using a large metal
spoon until well combined.

3 Roll teaspoons of the mixture into balls and place on the baking
trays. Using your thumb, make small indentations in the centre of
each biscuit, then spoon a little jam into each dent.

4 Bake for 12–15 minutes or until light golden brown. Transfer to
a wire rack to cool.

Melting moments

Sandwiched together with a gorgeous citrus icing, these melt-in-the-mouth biscuits are heavenly. Melting moments would make a delightful gift; store them in an airtight tin to keep them crisp.

125g soft butter
30g icing sugar, plus extra, for dusting
110g plain flour
30g cornflour

For the icing:
3 tbsp butter, at room temperature
85g icing sugar

2 tsp grated lemon or orange zest
1 tbsp lemon or orange juice

Makes: 12
Preparation: 20 minutes
Cooking: 15 minutes

1 Preheat the oven to 160°C (gas mark 3). Line two baking trays with baking parchment.

2 Using an electric mixer, beat the butter and icing sugar in a bowl until light and creamy. Sift the flour and cornflour over the mixture and stir until well combined.

3 With lightly floured hands, roll teaspoons of the dough into 24 small balls. Place on the baking trays and lightly press with a fork dipped in icing sugar. Bake for 15 minutes, or until the biscuits are just cooked through. Remove from the oven, transfer to a wire rack and leave to cool.

4 To make the icing, beat the butter, icing sugar and lemon or orange zest until smooth. Beat in the lemon or orange juice.

5 When the biscuits are cold, spread the icing over half the biscuits, then top with another biscuit.

Oat biscuits

Wholesome oats add goodness to these chewy, crumbly biscuits.
The coconut works well with the oat texture, and the butter and
syrup or treacle add a creamy, rich flavour.

150g butter, diced
115g caster sugar
2 tbsp golden syrup or black treacle
150g rolled oats
150g plain flour

45g desiccated coconut
1 tsp bicarbonate of soda

Makes: about 25
Preparation: 10 minutes
Cooking: 10–15 minutes

1 Preheat the oven to 160°C (gas mark 3). Line two baking trays
with baking parchment.

2 Combine the butter, sugar and golden syrup or black treacle
in a small saucepan over a medium heat. Stir until melted, then
remove from the heat. Mix the oats, flour and coconut together
in a bowl.

3 Combine the bicarbonate of soda with 1 tablespoon of boiling
water. Add to the butter mixture, then pour the butter mixture
over the dry ingredients and mix until well combined.

4 Spoon tablespoons of the mixture on to the baking trays.
Flatten them slightly with the back of a spoon, allowing room for
spreading. Bake for 10–15 minutes or until golden. Remove from
the oven and leave to cool on the baking trays.

Oatmeal and raisin cookies

Both children and adults will love these crisp melt-in-the-mouth cookies. Oatmeal is finely ground oats, so these cookies are a fairly healthy choice as well as tasting divine. The cookies freeze well.

85g soft butter, plus extra
for greasing
115g light muscovado sugar
1 egg, beaten
115g self-raising flour
55g medium oatmeal
170g raisins

Makes: about 18
Preparation time: 15 minutes
Cooking time: 10–15 minutes

1 Preheat the oven to 180°C (gas mark 4). Beat the butter and sugar together until light and creamy, then gradually beat in the egg. Sift in the flour, then fold it in with the oatmeal and raisins.

2 Drop heaped teaspoonfuls of the mixture on to three greased baking sheets, leaving enough space around each cookie to allow it to spread during baking.

3 Bake for 10–15 minutes or until golden brown. Cool slightly on the baking sheets, then transfer to a wire rack and leave to cool completely.

Cornish fairings

Traditionally, a "fairing" is any gift bought at a fair, and these light, delicious biscuits have been made for generations in Cornwall to sell at fairs. They are lightly spiced and crumbly.

70g butter
2 tbsp golden syrup
150g plain flour
1 level tsp bicarbonate of soda
1 tsp ground ginger
¼ tsp mixed spice
pinch of salt

grated zest of 1 lemon
25g golden caster sugar
sunflower oil, for greasing

Makes: 22
Preparation time: 15 minutes
Cooking time: 8 minutes

1 Heat the oven to 190°C (gas mark 5). Put the butter and syrup into a small saucepan and heat gently until the butter has melted. Remove from the heat and leave to cool for a couple of minutes.

2 Sift the flour, bicarbonate of soda, spices and salt into a bowl, then stir in the lemon zest and sugar. Add the warm butter mixture and mix gently but thoroughly.

3 Using your hands, and while the mixture is still soft and warm, pull off marble-sized pieces of the dough and roll into about 22 balls. Place on a greased baking sheet, spaced well apart, and using your fingers press each one down gently into a biscuit shape.

4 Bake for 8 minutes or until golden brown and still slightly soft in the middle. (They will firm up as they cool.) Remove to a wire rack to cool completely.

Gingersnaps

Thin, crisp and sweet, these ginger biscuits go well with tea. They spread slightly when cooking, so allow plenty of space on your baking tray. Gingersnaps are lovely with vanilla ice cream.

45g soft brown sugar
2 tbsp butter
2 tbsp golden syrup or black treacle
35g plain flour
1 tsp ground ginger

Makes: about 20
Preparation: 10 minutes
Cooking: 5–6 minutes

1 Preheat the oven to 180°C (gas mark 4). Line two baking trays with baking parchment.

2 Combine the sugar, butter and golden syrup or black treacle in a small saucepan over a medium heat and stir until the butter has melted. Remove from the heat. Sift the flour and ginger over the mixture and stir until combined.

3 Place teaspoons of the mixture on the baking trays, allowing room for spreading. Bake for 5–6 minutes, or until lightly golden. Remove from the oven and leave on the trays for 1–2 minutes, or until the biscuits harden. Transfer to a wire rack to cool.

Gingerbread men

Always a winner and so easy to make. Decorating them is almost as much fun as eating them and if you have a range of cutters, you can make a whole family of gingerbread people – and animals.

125g soft butter
115g caster sugar
1 egg
1 tbsp milk
375g plain flour, plus extra for dusting
1 tsp bicarbonate of soda
3 tsp ground ginger
2 tbsp golden syrup or black treacle

To decorate:
icing and coloured sweets,

Makes: 20
Preparation: 15 minutes, plus decorating time
Cooking: 15 minutes

1 Preheat the oven to 180°C (gas mark 4). Line two baking trays with baking parchment.

2 Using an electric mixer, beat the butter and sugar in a bowl until light and creamy. Add the egg and milk and beat until well combined.

3 Sift the flour, bicarbonate of soda and ginger over the butter mixture. Put the golden syrup in a microwave-safe jug and microwave on high for 10 to 20 seconds, or until warm. Add to the butter mixture and stir until well combined.

4 Turn the dough out on to a lightly floured surface and knead gently. Roll the dough between two sheets of baking parchment or greaseproof paper until 3mm thick. Using small gingerbread men cutters, cut out shapes from the dough and place on the baking trays, with a little space between each one.

5 Bake for 15 minutes, or until golden and firm to the touch. Remove from the oven and leave to cool on the trays. Decorate as desired, using icing and sweets.

Shrewsbury biscuits

Traditional to Shrewsbury for at least three hundred years, these biscuits have soft, chewy centres studded with currants. Some recipes also include a teaspoon of nutmeg, cinnamon or caraway seeds.

115g soft butter, plus extra for greasing
115g golden caster sugar, plus extra for dusting
1 egg, beaten
225g plain flour, plus extra for dusting
55g currants

grated zest of 1 lemon
sunflower oil, for greasing

Makes: 30
Preparation time: 20 minutes, plus 30 minutes resting
Cooking time: 15 minutes

1 Cream the butter and sugar together in a bowl until light and creamy.

2 Beat in the egg, a little at a time. Sift in the flour, then add the currants and lemon zest and mix well.

3 With lightly floured hands, bring the mixture together and turn it out on to a floured board. Roll out gently to a thickness of about 5mm. Using a round pastry cutter, about 5cm in diameter, stamp out about 30 rounds.

4 Place the rounds on two greased baking sheets and refrigerate for about 30 minutes, until firm. Meanwhile, preheat the oven to 180°C (gas mark 4).

5 Bake for 15 minutes or until firm to the touch. Transfer to a wire rack and dust lightly with caster sugar. Leave to cool.

Fig rolls

Here's a classic – a crisp, shortbread biscuit wrapped around a fig
and lemon filling. Less fiddly to make than you might think,
fig rolls are really delicious when homemade. Do give them a try.

115g plain white flour, plus
extra for dusting
115g plain wholemeal flour
150g butter, diced, plus extra
for greasing
65g light muscovado sugar
1 tsp vanilla extract
2 egg yolks

250g ready-to-eat dried figs,
finely chopped
2 tbsp lemon juice

Makes: 20
Preparation time: 35 minutes,
plus 30 minutes chilling
Cooking time: 12–15 minutes

1 Sift the white and wholemeal flours into a mixing bowl, tipping
in any bran left in the sieve. Rub in the butter with your fingertips
until the mixture resembles fine breadcrumbs.

2 Add the sugar, vanilla extract and egg yolks, and mix to a firm
dough, adding 1–2 teaspoons of water if necessary to bind.
Alternatively, blend the flours and butter in a food processor, then
add the sugar, vanilla and egg yolks, and blend briefly to make a
dough. Wrap in clingfilm and chill for 30 minutes.

3 Put the figs in a small, heavy-based saucepan with 6 tablespoons
of water. Bring to the boil, then reduce the heat, cover and simmer
gently for 3–5 minutes or until the figs have plumped up slightly
and absorbed the water. Transfer to a bowl and mash lightly with
a fork to break up the pieces. Add the lemon juice and stir, then
leave to cool.

4 Preheat the oven to 190°C (gas mark 5). Roll out the dough on
a lightly floured surface to a 50 x 15 cm rectangle. Cut the dough
rectangle in half lengthways to make two strips.

5 Spoon half the fig purée evenly along each strip, near to one of the long sides. Bring the opposite long side up and over the filling to form a log shape, and lightly press the edges of the dough together to seal.

6 Flatten each of the logs slightly. Using a sharp knife, cut each log across into 10 biscuits and transfer to a greased baking sheet. Prick each biscuit with a fork or score with a sharp knife. Bake for 12–15 minutes or until slightly darkened in colour.

7 Transfer the biscuits to a wire rack to cool.

Chocolate chip cookies

The rich chocolate chip must be one of the most universally popular cookies of all time. Once they are out of the oven, watch them disappear in double-quick time.

125g soft butter, plus extra for greasing
80g caster sugar
1 tsp vanilla extract
2 tbsp condensed milk
150g self-raising flour

125g dark chocolate, chopped
sifted icing sugar, for dusting

Makes: about 30
Preparation: 15 minutes
Cooking: 15 minutes

1 Preheat the oven to 160°C (gas mark 3). Grease two baking trays and line with baking parchment.

2 Using an electric mixer, beat the butter, sugar and vanilla extract in a bowl until light and creamy. Add the condensed milk and mix well. Fold the flour and chocolate into the butter mixture.

3 Spoon half-tablespoons of the mixture on to the baking trays, allowing room for spreading. Bake for 15 minutes. Remove from the oven and leave to cool on the trays for 3 minutes, then carefully transfer to a wire rack and allow to cool completely.

4 Lightly dust with icing sugar.

Savouries

Souffléd salmon tartlets

Individual tartlets are a traditional option for the start of a full afternoon tea or make a more substantial meal served with salad. The pastry and souffléd salmon of these tartlets are very light.

For the pastry:
125g plain flour
55g butter, diced, plus extra
for greasing

For the filling:
25g cornflour
170ml milk
180g tinned skinless, boneless
pink salmon, drained
and flaked
2 tbsp chopped fresh dill
2 tbsp chopped fresh chives
2 eggs, separated

To serve:
175g mixed salad leaves, such
as frisée and rocket
1 red pepper, seeds removed,
cut into thin strips

Serves: 6
Preparation time: 40 minutes,
plus 30 minutes chilling
Cooking time: 15 minutes

1 Sift the flour into a large bowl. Add the butter and using your fingertips, rub in until the mixture resembles fine breadcrumbs. Sprinkle over 2 tablespoons of cold water and mix to form a dough. Gather into a smooth ball, wrap in clingfilm and chill for at least 30 minutes.

2 Blend the cornflour with 2 tablespoons of milk to make a smooth paste. Heat the remaining milk to boiling point and pour a little into the cornflour mixture, stirring. Add the mixture to the milk in the pan. Bring to the boil and stir until the sauce thickens. Reduce the heat and leave to simmer gently for 2 minutes.

3 Remove the pan from the heat. Stir in salmon, dill and chives; add salt and black pepper to taste. Mix in the egg yolks. Set aside.

4 Preheat the oven to 200°C (gas mark 6). Grease six 9cm non-stick loose-base tartlet tins with butter. Divide the pastry into six pieces, and roll out each piece thinly to line the tartlet tins.

5 Prick the pastry cases several times with a fork, and place the tins on a baking sheet. Line the tins with baking parchment and fill with dried beans to weigh down the pastry. Cook for 10 minutes, then remove the paper and beans. Bake for a further 5 minutes or until the pastry is lightly golden. Allow to cool, then carefully remove the tartlet cases from the tins and replace them on the baking sheet.

6 Whisk the egg whites until stiff and fold into the salmon mixture. Spoon the mixture into cases and bake for 15 minutes or until well risen and golden. Serve warm on individual plates, with the salad leaves and strips of red pepper.

Cheese and watercress scones

Peppery watercress and mature Cheddar cheese flavour these nutritious savoury scones. Serve them warm with butter for a delicious start to afternoon tea, or with soup for lunch or supper.

125g self-raising flour, plus extra for dusting
150g self-raising wholemeal flour
1 tsp baking powder
3 tbsp butter, diced, plus extra for greasing
50g rolled oats

85g watercress leaves, chopped
75g mature Cheddar cheese, grated
125ml milk, plus extra to glaze

Makes: 8
Preparation time: 20 minutes
Cooking time: 10–15 minutes

1 Preheat the oven to 230°C (gas mark 8). Sift the flours and baking powder into a bowl and tip in any bran left in the sieve. Rub in the butter using your fingertips until the mixture resembles fine breadcrumbs.

2 Add the rolled oats, watercress and about three-quarters of the cheese. Season with salt and black pepper, and stir in the milk using a fork. Scrape the dough together and turn out on to a well-floured work surface. Shape into a smooth, soft ball.

3 Pat or roll out the dough to 2cm thick. Use a 7.5cm round cutter to stamp out scones. Press the trimmings together lightly to re-roll and stamp out more scones.

4 Grease a large baking tray. Place the scones on the baking tray, arranging them so they are not touching. Brush the tops lightly with milk and sprinkle with the remaining grated cheese. Bake for 10–15 minutes or until risen and golden brown. Cool on a wire rack.

Red onion pastries

Very simple to make, these tasty red onion pastries make a pretty savoury start to afternoon tea. The red onion caramelises slightly during baking to give a lovely sweet flavour.

2 sheets ready-rolled puff
pastry, thawed (about 300g)
1 egg
2 small red onions, peeled and
thinly sliced
4 large shallots, peeled and
quartered

12 sprigs thyme
4 tablespoons olive oil, plus
  extra for greasing

Makes: 4
Preparation time: 30 minutes
Cooking time: 20 minutes

1 Preheat the oven to 220°C (gas mark 7). On a floured work surface, roll out each piece of pastry to a rectangle of about 30 x 15cm. Cut two large rounds from each, using a 13–15cm saucer as a guide. Grease a large baking tray with olive oil, and place the pastry rounds on it.

2 Beat the egg lightly and brush over the pastry, taking care not to let any trickle over the edges.

3 Divide the onions and shallots between the rounds, placing a mound in the centre of each one; leave a border of about 2cm all round. Place three sprigs of thyme on the top of each mound.

4 Brush the onion mixture with a little olive oil and season to taste with salt and black pepper. Bake for 20 minutes or until the pastries have puffed up and are golden brown.

Spicy potato and leek quiche

For a more substantial afternoon meal, this tasty quiche can be prepared in advance and served warm or chilled. The heat and flavour of the red chillies works well with the Gruyère cheese.

For the pastry:
170g plain flour, plus extra for dusting
pinch of salt
2 fresh red chillies, seeds removed, finely chopped
2 tsp chopped fresh thyme
1 egg
80ml sunflower oil
1 tbsp lukewarm water

For the filling:
350g waxy new potatoes
250g leeks, cut into 1cm slices
65g Gruyère cheese, grated
2 tbsp chopped chives
55g rocket, roughly chopped
2 eggs
150ml milk

Serves: 4–8
Preparation time: 30 minutes plus 30 minutes resting
Cooking time: 40–45 minutes

1 Sift the flour and a pinch of salt into a large bowl. Add the chilli and thyme, then make a well in the centre. Whisk the egg, oil and water and add to the dry ingredients; mix well with a fork and bring everything together to make a dough.

2 Place the dough on a lightly floured work surface and knead briefly until smooth. Place in a dry bowl, cover with a damp tea towel and leave to rest for about 30 minutes before rolling out.

3 For the filling, cook the potatoes in boiling water for 10–12 minutes or until almost tender. Steam leeks over the potatoes for 6–7 minutes, until tender. Drain thoroughly and leave until cool enough to handle.

4 Preheat the oven to 200°C (gas mark 6) and put a baking tray in to heat. On a lightly floured work surface, roll out the pastry thinly to line a 20cm round, fluted loose-based quiche tin.

5 Scatter half the cheese in the case. Thickly slice the potatoes and toss with the leeks, remaining cheese and chives. Season with salt and pepper. Arrange half the potato and leek mixture in the pastry case. Scatter the rocket on top, then add the rest of the potato and leek mixture.

6 Lightly beat the eggs in a jug. Heat the milk to just below boiling point, then add to the eggs; whisk gently to combine.

7 Place the tin on the hot baking tray. Pour the warm egg custard into the case. Bake for 10 minutes, then reduce oven temperature to 180°C (gas mark 4) and bake for a further 30–35 minutes or until the filling is lightly set. Leave quiche in the tin for 5 minutes. Serve warm or chilled.

Bacon and onion tart

Just a small amount of good quality bacon adds a lot of flavour to this delicious tart. The sprinkling of caraway seeds adds another dimension. This is lovely served warm or chilled.

For the pastry:
250g plain flour
2 tsp dried yeast
125ml lukewarm milk
1 tbsp butter
¼ tsp salt

For the filling:
125g butter, plus extra
for greasing
2 kilos red onions, thinly sliced

2 eggs
55g bacon, finely diced
¼ tsp caraway seeds
3 egg yolks
185ml cream

Serves: 8
Preparation time: 45 minutes
plus 1¼ hours resting
Cooking time: 1 hour

1 Grease a 28cm springform tin. Place the flour in a bowl and make a well in the centre. Sprinkle the yeast on to the milk and pour the milk into the well. Stir in to combine. Cover and leave to rise in a warm place for 15 minutes.

2 Add the 1 tablespoon of the butter and the salt, then knead into a dough. Cover and leave to rise in a warm place for 30 minutes. Knead for 10 minutes, then leave to rise again for 30 minutes.

3 Preheat the oven to 220°C (gas mark 7). In a frying pan, heat the butter and fry the onion until transparent. Whisk the eggs in a bowl, then stir in onions.

4 Roll out the dough to line the tin. Pour in the onion mixture and sprinkle with the bacon and caraway seeds. Bake for 10 minutes, then reduce the oven temperature to 180°C (gas mark 4).

5 Meanwhile, combine the egg yolks, a pinch of salt and the cream. Pour this mixture over the tart, and bake for 50 minutes. Leave to cool slightly before removing carefully from the tin.

Quiche Lorraine

Probably the most well-known quiche, this classic from the
Lorraine region of France contains bacon or ham and creamy
Emmental or Gruyère cheese. Serve thin slices for afternoon tea.

For the pastry:
200g plain flour, plus extra
for dusting
120g butter, diced, plus extra
for greasing
1 egg yolk

For the filling:
160g sour cream
3 eggs and 1 egg yolk
pinch of grated nutmeg

150g ham or bacon, sliced
200g Emmental or Gruyère
cheese, grated
salt and black pepper, to taste

Serves: 6
Preparation time: 35 minutes,
plus 30 minutes chilling
Cooking time: 42–52 minutes

1 Grease a 26cm springform tin with butter. Place the flour,
butter, egg yolk, a pinch of salt and 2 tablespoons of water in
a bowl. Knead into a smooth dough. Shape into a ball, wrap in
clingfilm and chill for 30 minutes.

2 Preheat the oven to 180°C (gas mark 4). Roll the dough out on a
lightly floured work surface and use to line the tin; the side of
pastry case should be about 5cm high.

3 Prick the pastry base several times with a fork, cover with baking
parchment and dried beans and bake for 12 minutes. Remove the
baking parchment and dried beans and cook the base for a further
5 minutes. Remove from oven and leave to cool slightly.

4 To make the filling, combine the sour cream with the eggs, egg
yolk and nutmeg, and season with black pepper and a little salt.

5 Spread the ham or bacon over the pastry base. Sprinkle over the
cheese. Pour in the egg mixture, then bake for 25–35 minutes.
Leave to cool slightly before removing carefully from the tin.

Broccoli quiche with salmon

Delicious broccoli, salmon and dill make this ideal for a summer afternoon tea. Both the dough and filling use low-fat sour cream, which gives a subtle flavour that works well with the rich salmon.

For the dough:
100g low-fat sour cream
2 eggs
1 tsp sunflower oil, plus extra for greasing
220g plain flour, plus extra for dusting
1 tsp dried yeast

For the filling:
600g broccoli
200g low-fat sour cream
3 eggs

1 tbsp cornflour
20g finely chopped dill
pinch of grated nutmeg
1 tsp grated horseradish, optional
1–2 tsp lemon juice
200g smoked salmon, sliced

Serves: 8
Preparation time: 45 minutes, plus 30 minutes rising
Cooking time: 35–45 minutes

1 To make the dough, mix the sour cream, eggs, oil and a pinch of salt in a bowl until smooth. Combine the flour and dry yeast and add to sour cream mixture. Knead into a sticky dough. Cover the bowl with clingfilm and leave the dough to rise in a warm place for 30 minutes.

2 Separate the florets from the broccoli stems. Peel the thick stems thinly and cut into large pieces.

3 Place the florets and stems in a steamer and cook for about 8 minutes. Remove the florets from the steamer and set aside. Mash the stems finely in a mixing bowl with some of the cooking water, and leave to cool.

4 Whisk together the sour cream, eggs and cornflour, then stir in the dill. Stir the mixture into the broccoli purée. Add the nutmeg, horseradish and lemon juice and season with salt and pepper.

5 Preheat the oven to 200°C (gas mark 6). Grease a 28cm ceramic fluted quiche dish with sunflower oil. On a lightly floured work surface, roll out the pastry to line the dish. Spread the broccoli florets and strips of salmon over the pastry base and pour the filling mixture over the top.

6 Bake the quiche for 35–45 minutes until the pastry is crisp and the filling slightly browned. Serve warm.

Cheese and tomato rarebit

A classic for afternoon tea, this is the tastiest cheese on toast you could wish for. There are many versions of Welsh rarebit (or rabbit); this one includes breadcrumbs to add texture.

90ml semi-skimmed milk
dash of Worcestershire sauce
125g mature Cheddar cheese, grated
40g fresh wholemeal breadcrumbs
4 thick slices wholemeal bread
4 firm but ripe tomatoes, thinly sliced

Serves: 4
Preparation time: 15 minutes, plus 5 minutes standing
Cooking time: 4–5 minutes

1 Preheat the grill to high. Put the milk, Worcestershire sauce and cheese in a small heavy-based saucepan and stir over a gentle heat until the cheese has melted and the mixture is smooth. Remove from the heat and stir in the breadcrumbs. Cool for 3–4 minutes, stirring occasionally, until the topping has thickened to a spreading consistency.

2 Meanwhile, arrange the slices of bread on a baking tray and toast on both sides under the grill.

3 Top the toast with the slices of tomato, then spoon over the cheese mixture, spreading it out to cover the toast completely. Return to the grill and cook for 2–3 minutes or until the cheese mixture is golden brown and bubbling.

Warm potted shrimps

Potted shrimps have been popular in the north of England since the 18th century. Shrimps come from Morecambe Bay in Lancashire. These pots are delicious with hot toast.

175g butter
450g peeled shrimps
¼ tsp powdered mace
¼ tsp cayenne pepper

Serves: 4
Preparation time: 20 minutes
Cooking time: 10 minutes

To serve:
4 slices of hot toast
1 lemon, cut into wedges

1 Melt 125g of the butter over a moderate heat. Add the shrimps, mace and Cayenne pepper. Season with salt and pepper. Heat thoroughly, but do not allow the shrimps to boil as this toughens them. Stir them as they cook.

2 Spoon the shrimps and butter into four small pots or ramekins.

3 Meanwhile, melt the remaining butter in a saucepan. Skim off the foam as the butter heats. Remove the pan from the heat and let the sediment sink to the bottom. Strain the butter through a muslin cloth. Allow the liquid to cool a little before pouring it over the shrimps in each pot.

4 Just before serving, place the pots in a saucepan of simmering water and heat for 2–3 minutes. Invert each pot of shrimps on to a plate. Serve with hot toast and wedges of lemon to squeeze over.

Scrambled eggs with smoked salmon

A British classic, which can be served on toast for high tea. Choose a good granary or sourdough bread for crunchy toast. The addition of double cream makes this very rich and luxurious.

7 eggs
3 tbsp double cream
100g smoked salmon, sliced
75g butter
6 slices of hot, buttered toast, to serve
6 sprigs parsley, to garnish

Serves: 6
Preparation time: 8 minutes
Cooking time: 2–3 minutes

1 Beat the eggs lightly and stir in the cream and smoked salmon.

2 Melt the butter in a large, heavy-based pan over a low heat and pour in the egg and salmon mixture. Stir gently and continuously for 2–3 minutes until the eggs are lightly set and creamy. Season to taste with salt and black pepper.

3 Remove the pan from the heat and quickly arrange the soft scrambled eggs over slices of hot, buttered toast. Garnish with the sprigs of parsley and serve.

Mushroom and thyme toasts

The rich flavour of chestnut mushrooms is enhanced by cooking them with garlic, herbs and a dollop of tangy crème fraîche, and they taste wonderful piled on top of toast.

125 g ricotta cheese
2 celery sticks, finely chopped
3 tbsp finely chopped parsley
good pinch of cayenne pepper
500 g chestnut mushrooms
1 garlic clove, crushed
2 tbsp chopped fresh thyme
2 tbsp crème fraîche

1 tsp lemon juice
8 thick slices cut from a small
  loaf of mixed seed bread

Serves: 4
Preparation: 10 minutes
Cooking time: 8 minutes

1 Put the ricotta, celery, parsley and cayenne pepper in a bowl and mix well together. Set aside in a cool place until needed. Preheat the grill to high.

2 Leave any small mushrooms whole and halve larger ones. Place them in a large, heavy frying pan, preferably non-stick, and add the garlic, thyme, crème fraîche and 1 teaspoon of water. Cover and cook gently for 3–4 minutes or until the mushrooms are just tender and have released their juices. Add the lemon juice and season with salt and pepper to taste.

3 While the mushrooms are cooking, toast the bread slices on both sides under the grill. While still warm, spread one side of each piece of toast with some of the ricotta mixture, then cut them in half.

4 Arrange the toasts on individual serving plates. Spoon the hot mushroom mixture over the toasts and serve immediately.

Potted ham

This is a good way of using up leftover ham. Originally potting with clarified butter was a way of preserving meats and fish. This recipe is simpler, and will last just a few days in the fridge.

275g cooked ham
pinch each of dried marjoram,
thyme and mace
75g butter

Serves: 4
Preparation time: 10 minutes
Cooking time: 5 minutes, plus
chilling

To serve:
8–12 oatcakes or slices of toast
a few tbsp of piccalilli

1 Chop the ham and put it through the fine blade of a mincer twice. Season to taste with the marjoram, thyme, mace, and salt and pepper.

2 Melt 50g of the butter in a small saucepan and add the ham. Heat gently together for about 5 minutes. Pack the meat into an earthenware jar or pot and set aside to cool.

3 Heat the remaining butter until foaming, strain through a muslin cloth or fine sieve and pour over the meat. Leave the pot in the refrigerator to set.

4 Serve the potted ham with oatcakes or slices of hot toast, and a spoonful of piccalilli for each person.

Pies
and tarts

Cherry streudel

This melt-in-the-mouth pastry is packed with fresh, juicy cherries. The ground almonds and breadcrumbs in the filling absorb the fruit juices, to keep the pastry crisp.

For the filling:
30g fresh white breadcrumbs
55g ground almonds
45g soft light brown sugar
grated zest of 1 orange
675g fresh cherries, stoned, and halved if large

For the pastry:
3 sheets filo pastry, each 30 x 50cm

30g butter, melted, plus extra for greasing
15g flaked almonds
1 tbsp icing sugar, sifted

Serves: 6
Preparation time: 20 minutes
Cooking time: 20 minutes

1 Preheat the oven to 200°C (gas mark 6). To make the filling, stir the breadcrumbs, ground almonds, brown sugar and orange zest together in a large bowl. Add the cherries and mix well.

2 Lay a sheet of filo pastry out on a clean tea towel and brush very lightly with melted butter. Place a second sheet of filo on top and brush very lightly with butter. Repeat with the third sheet.

3 Spoon the filling evenly over the pastry, leaving a 2.5cm margin clear around the edges. Turn in the edges on the short side.

4 With the help of the tea towel, roll up from a long side to make a thick sausage shape. Transfer to a lightly greased, non-stick baking tray, with the seam side underneath. Brush with the remaining butter and scatter the flaked almonds over.

5 Bake for 20 minutes or until the pastry and almonds are golden brown. Dust with the icing sugar and serve warm or cold.

Pear and almond tart

A patisserie favourite, made with pears baked in an almond
frangipane filling.

For the pastry:	2 egg yolks
75g butter, diced	25g plain flour
150g plain flour, sifted, plus	50g ground almonds
extra for dusting	411g canned pear halves in
pinch of salt	juice, drained
For the filling:	**Serves:** 6
50g butter	**Preparation time:** 35 minutes
50g caster sugar	**Cooking time:** 40 minutes

1 To make the pastry, rub the butter into the flour and salt with
your fingertips until the mixture resembles fine breadcrumbs.
Sprinkle over 2–3 tablespoons of cold water, then bind the
mixture together. Knead lightly to form a dough. Wrap the pastry
in clingfilm and chill in the fridge for 20 minutes.

2 Preheat the oven to 200°C (gas mark 6) and put a baking sheet
in to heat. Roll out the pastry on a lightly floured surface and
use to line a 24cm loose-based fluted tart tin. Prick the base all
over. Place the tart case on the baking sheet, line with baking
parchment and dried beans and bake for 10 minutes. Lift out the
beans and paper, and return to the oven for a further 5 minutes.

3 Meanwhile, make the filling. Cream together the butter and
sugar until light and creamy. Beat in the egg yolks, followed by
the flour and ground almonds. Cut the pear halves into parallel
slices, but do not separate.

4 Spread the almond mixture over the base of the tart. Place each
pear half in the tart tin, with the pointed ends towards the centre.

5 Bake the tart for 25 minutes until golden and firm. Leave to cool
slightly before removing from the tin.

Blueberry cheesecake

Compared to most cheesecakes, this version isn't particularly high in fat, as it uses cottage and curd cheeses instead of cream cheese, and is lightened by folding in whisked egg whites before baking.

115g digestive biscuits
2 tbsp jumbo oats
55g butter, melted
200g cottage cheese
200g curd cheese
4 tbsp fromage frais
1 whole egg
2 eggs, separated
4 tsp cornflour
grated zest of 1 lemon

115g icing sugar, sifted
140g blueberries

To decorate:
55g blueberries
fresh mint leaves
1 tbsp icing sugar, sifted

Serves: 8
Preparation time: 25 minutes
Cooking time: 1½ hours

1 Preheat the oven to 180°C (gas mark 4). Line the bottom of a 21cm springform cake tin with baking parchment.

2 Make the biscuits into crumbs, either by crushing them in a food processor or by putting them in a strong plastic bag and crushing them with a rolling pin.

3 Mix together the crushed biscuits, oats and melted butter. Spread this mixture evenly over the bottom of the prepared tin, pressing down firmly, and set aside.

4 Put the cottage cheese in a food processor or blender and blend until smooth. Add the curd cheese, fromage frais, the whole egg, 2 egg yolks, cornflour and lemon zest. Blend briefly until evenly mixed. Spoon the mixture into a bowl.

5 Whisk the 2 egg whites in a clean bowl until they form soft peaks. Add the icing sugar gradually. Gently fold half the meringue into the cheese mixture, then fold in the blueberries, followed by the rest of the meringue.

6 Pour the mixture over the biscuit base in the tin and bake for 30 minutes. Cover loosely with foil and reduce the oven temperature to 160°C (gas mark 3). Bake for a further 1 hour or until the cheesecake feels just set in the centre. Turn off the oven and leave the cheesecake inside to cool for 30 minutes, with the door slightly ajar – this helps to prevent cracking.

7 Transfer the cheesecake to a wire rack to cool completely, then chill until ready to serve. Run a knife around the side of the cheesecake to loosen it, then remove it from the tin. Peel off the lining paper and place the cheesecake on a serving plate. Decorate with the extra blueberries and a few fresh mint leaves, and finish with a light dusting of icing sugar.

Meringue-topped berry tartlets

Make these irresistible tartlets in summer when redcurrants and
blackcurrants are in season. The tartlet cases are made with a light
almond pastry and are topped with crisp meringue.

For the pastry:
85g plain flour, plus extra for
dusting
30g ground almonds
55g butter, diced
25g icing sugar, sifted
1 egg yolk

For the filling:
200g redcurrants
200g blackcurrants
2 tbsp caster sugar

125g strawberries, chopped
1 tbsp redcurrant jelly

For the meringue topping:
2 egg whites
55g caster sugar

Serves: 6
Preparation: 30 minutes, plus
30 minutes chilling
Cooking time: 35 minutes

1 To make the pastry, sift the flour into a mixing bowl and stir
in the ground almonds. Add the butter and rub in using your
fingertips until the mixture resembles fine breadcrumbs. Stir in
the sugar.

2 Lightly beat the egg yolk with 1 tablespoon of cold water. Add
to the flour mixture and mix in with a round-bladed knife. Gather
together to make a soft dough. Wrap in clingfilm and chill for at
least 30 minutes before rolling out.

3 Preheat the oven to 190°C (gas mark 5). To make the filling, put
the redcurrants and blackcurrants in a saucepan with the caster
sugar and cook very gently for 5 minutes or until the currants are
softened but still holding their shape. Remove from the heat and
stir in the strawberries and redcurrant jelly. Set aside.

4 Roll out the pastry dough thinly on a lightly floured work
surface. Use to line six individual, loose-bottomed, non-stick

tartlet tins (9 x 2.5 cm deep). Prick the tartlet cases and place on a baking sheet. Line the cases with baking parchment and dried beans, and bake for 10 minutes, then remove the paper and beans. Bake for a further 2–3 minutes or until light golden. Remove the tartlet cases from the oven and set aside to cool. Reduce the oven temperature to 160°C (gas mark 3).

5 Meanwhile, make the meringue topping. Whisk the egg whites until stiff, then gradually whisk in the caster sugar to make a thick, glossy meringue.

6 Carefully remove the pastry cases from the tins and place back on the baking sheet. Drain the fruit using a slotted spoon, then fill the pastry cases with the fruit.

7 Top the tartlets with the meringue, swirling it gently to cover the fruit completely. Bake for 10–15 minutes or until the meringue is set and lightly golden. Serve warm or cold.

Latticed apple pie

The lattice pattern is a classic decoration for shortcrust pies; you
can see the baked fruit filling through the pastry.

For the pastry:
250g plain flour
½ tsp baking powder
150g butter, plus extra for
greasing
2 tbsp honey
2 egg yolks

For the filling:
6 apples, about 600g in total
1 tsp lemon juice

125ml cream
2 eggs
3 egg yolks
1 tsp vanilla extract
3 tbsp sugar
70g ground almonds

Serves: 10–12
Preparation time: 45 minutes,
plus 50 minutes chilling
Cooking time: 30 minutes

1 To make the pastry, sift the flour and baking powder into a
bowl. Add the butter, honey, egg yolks and water and knead to
form a dough. Wrap in clingfilm and chill for 30 minutes.

2 Set one-fifth of pastry aside. Grease a 26cm springform tin with
butter. Roll out the rest of the pastry to line the tin, making an
edge 2.5cm high. Prick the base with a fork. Chill for 20 minutes.

3 Preheat the oven to 180°C (gas mark 4). Cover the pastry base
with baking parchment and dried beans. Bake for 10 minutes,
then remove the baking parchment and beans. Meanwhile, peel,
core and slice the apples. Drizzle with the lemon juice.

4 For the filling, set 1 tbsp of cream aside and mix remaining
cream, eggs, 2 of the egg yolks, vanilla, sugar and almonds
together. Fill the pastry case with the apples and pour the cream
mixture over.

5 Increase the oven temperature to 200°C (gas mark 6). Cut the
saved pastry into thin strips and arrange on top in a lattice. Brush
with the remaining egg yolk and bake for 20 minutes.

Richmond maids of honour

These dainty little curd tarts were named after the maids who served Henry VIII at Richmond Palace. You can buy them at the Original Maids of Honour teashop near Richmond.

sunflower oil, for greasing
225g ready-rolled puff pastry
225g curd cheese
1 egg
grated zest of 1 lemon
15g butter, melted
55g golden caster sugar

Makes: 12
Preparation time: 30 minutes, plus 1 hour chilling
Cooking time: 30–40 minutes

1 Preheat the oven to 200°C (gas mark 6) and grease a muffin or bun tin with sunflower oil. Lay the pastry out on a floured board and, using a pastry cutter or glass, stamp out 12 rounds, each about 7.5cm in diameter.

2 Press the pastry rounds into the prepared tin and chill in the fridge for about 1 hour.

3 Put the curd cheese, egg, lemon zest, butter and sugar in a bowl and beat together. Divide the mixture between the chilled pastry shells and bake for 30–40 minutes or until the filling is puffed up and golden.

4 Remove the tarts from the tin to a wire rack to cool a little. Serve warm.

Treacle tart

A classic British "nursery" pud, treacle tart was originally a way of using leftover bread. You mix day-old breadcrumbs with golden syrup to make the delicious filling.

For the pastry:
225g plain flour
100g butter, diced
3 tbsp iced water

For the filling:
350g golden syrup
25g butter
1 tsp finely grated lemon zest
2 tbsp lemon juice
½ tsp ground ginger

160g fresh white breadcrumbs, made from day-old bread
1 egg, lightly beaten
clotted cream or ice cream, to serve

Serves: 8
Preparation time: 20 minutes
Cooking time: 40 minutes

1 Preheat the oven to 180°C (gas mark 4).

2 To make the pastry, sift the flour into a large bowl. Using your fingertips, rub in the butter until the mixture resembles fine breadcrumbs. Add the iced water and mix with a flat-bladed knife until the mixture starts to clump together.

3 Turn the dough out on to a sheet of baking paper and gather into a ball. Set aside one-third of the dough. Roll out the remaining dough on the baking paper and use it to line a 20cm pie dish. Roll the other piece of dough to a 12 x 25cm rectangle, then cut into long strips 1cm wide.

4 To make the filling, put the golden syrup, butter, lemon zest, lemon juice and ground ginger in a small saucepan over medium heat. Stir until melted and combined. Place the breadcrumbs in a large bowl and pour the syrup mixture over. Stir well, then spoon into the pastry shell, spreading it to cover the pastry.

5 'Weave' the pastry strips over the pie. To do this, lay the first six strips over the pie, then fold every second one back. Lay one strip at right angles across the top, then fold the strips back. Fold the alternating strips back, and lay another strip across. Continue until all the strips are used. Trim any overhanging pastry, then press around the edges with a fork. Brush the pastry with beaten egg.

6 Bake for 40 minutes, or until the pastry is golden brown and the filling has browned. Cut into slices and serve warm with clotted cream or ice cream.

Lemon tart

Zesty and tangy, this lemon tart is perfect for afternoon tea in the summer. It is delicious served with a few summer berries.

For the pastry:
175g plain flour, plus extra for dusting
100g butter, diced
2 tbsp caster sugar
1 egg yolk

For the filling:
grated zest and juice of 2 lemons

115g butter, melted
3 eggs
150g caster sugar
25g plain flour, sifted
10g cornflour, sifted

Serves: 6
Preparation time: 30 minutes, plus 30 minutes chilling
Cooking time: 30 minutes

1 Sift the flour, then rub in the butter using your fingertips until the mixture resembles fine breadcrumbs. Stir in the sugar and a pinch of salt, then the egg yolk and 1 tablespoon of cold water, and mix to a firm dough. Wrap in clingfilm and leave to rest in the fridge for 20 minutes.

2 Preheat the oven to 190°C (gas mark 5). Put a baking sheet in to heat.

3 Roll out the pastry on a lightly floured surface to a thickness of 2mm and use to line a loose-based 24cm tart tin.

4 Prick the base all over with a fork and chill for a further 10 minutes.

5 Cover the pastry with baking parchment and dried beans. Place the tin on the baking sheet and bake for 12–15 minutes, until the pastry is set and pale golden. Remove the parchment and beans.

6 Meanwhile, make the filling. Mix together the lemon zest and juice, melted butter, eggs, sugar, flour and cornflour in a large bowl and beat until smooth.

7 Reduce the oven temperature to 180°C (gas mark 4). Pour in the lemon mixture and bake for 15 minutes or until the filling has set.

8 Leave to cool for 10 minutes before removing from the tin.

Index

A

almonds
boiled fruit cake 14
cherry and almond
cake 26
cherry streudel 112
chocolate muffins 63
cinnamon star
biscuits 82
Dundee cake 10
honey cake 32
latticed apple pie 118
macaroons 80
meringue-topped berry
tartlets 116–117
pear and almond
tart 113
seed cake 15
Spanish orange and
almond cake 30–31
Anglesey cake 11
apples
latticed apple pie 118
Somerset apple cake 33
apricots: flapjacks with
apricots 74

B

bacon
bacon and onion tart 102
quiche lorraine 103
bananas
banana cake 23
flapjacks with
apricots 74
Bara brith 45
barm brack 46–47
Bath buns 50–51
blackberry and lemon
scones 59

blackcurrants
blackcurrant fruit
loaf 42
meringue-topped berry
tartlets 116–117
black treacle
Anglesey cake 11
gingerbread men 90
gingersnaps 89
oat biscuits 86
rich chocolate cake with
fudge icing 36–37
Somerset apple cake 33
spiced oatmeal parkin 49
treacle gingerbread
loaf 48
blueberries
blueberry cheesecake
114–115
blueberry muffins 62
Scotch pancakes 76–77
broccoli quiche with
salmon 104–105

C

carrot and Brazil nut
cake 24–25
cheese
blueberry cheesecake
114–115
cheese and tomato
rarebit 106
cheese and watercress
scones 98
quiche lorraine 103
Richmond maids of
honour 119
spicy potato and leek
quiche 100–101
see also fromage frais;
ricotta cheese

Chelsea buns 54–55
cherries
boiled fruit cake 14
cherry and almond
cake 26
cherry streudel 112
chocolate cherry
slice 68
Dundee cake 10
rich fruit ring
cake 12–13
chocolate
chocolate brownies 64
chocolate cherry
slice 68
chocolate chip
cookies 94
chocolate coconut
squares 65
chocolate éclairs 60–61
chocolate muffins 63
chocolate peppermint
slice 67
rich chocolate cake with
fudge icing 36–37
rich chocolate torte 38
Chorley cakes 72–73
cinnamon
cinnamon raisin
bread 43
cinnamon star
biscuits 82
cinnamon teacake 53
coconut
chocolate cherry
slice 68
chocolate coconut
squares 65
coconut macaroons 81
jam and coconut slice 66
oat biscuits 86
coffee walnut cake 22

Cornish fairings 88
cream
  chocolate éclairs
    60–61
  Genoese sponge cake 17
  meringues 78
  strawberry shortcake
    34–35
  see also sour cream

D

dates
  boiled fruit cake 14
  cold tea cake 16
  date and walnut loaf 27
  rich fruit ring cake
    12–13
dried fruit
  Anglesey cake 11
  banana cake 23
  Bara brith 45
  barm brack 46–47
  Bath buns 50–51
  big fruity tea bun 40–41
  boiled fruit cake 14
  carrot and Brazil nut
    cake 24–25
  Chelsea buns 54–55
  Chorley cakes 72–73
  cinnamon raisin
    bread 43
  cold tea cake 16
  Dundee cake 10
  just-right rock cakes 70
  malted sultana bread 44
  oatmeal and raisin
    cookies 87
  rich fruit ring cake 12–13
  Shrewsbury biscuits 91
  teacakes 52
Dundee cake 10

F

figs
  fig rolls 92–93
  rich fruit ring cake
    12–13
fish and seafood
  broccoli quiche with
    salmon 104–105
  scrambled eggs with
    smoked salmon 108
  souffléd salmon tartlets
    96–97
  warm potted shrimps 107
flapjacks with apricots 74
fromage frais
  blueberry cheesecake
    114–115
  Scotch pancakes 76–77

G

Genoese sponge cake 17
ginger
  Anglesey cake 11
  Cornish fairings 88
  gingerbread men 90
  gingersnaps 89
  rich fruit ring cake
    12–13
  spiced oatmeal
    parkin 49
  treacle gingerbread
    loaf 48
Grandma's never-fail
  sponge 18

H

ham
  potted ham 110
  quiche lorraine 103
hazelnuts

hazelnut meringue
  cake 28–29
rich fruit ring cake 12–13
honey
  flapjacks with apricots 74
  honey cake 32
  latticed apple pie 118
  malted sultana bread 44
  Scotch pancakes 76–77

J

jam
  chocolate coconut
    squares 65
  Genoese sponge cake 17
  jam and coconut slice 66
  jam drop biscuits 84
  Victoria sandwich 20

K

Kentish huffkins 56

L

leeks: spicy potato and
  leek quiche 100–101
lemons
  blackberry and lemon
    scones 59
  lemon slice 69
  lemon tart 122–123
  melting moments 85

M

macaroons 80
  coconut macaroons 81
Madeira cake 21
malted sultana bread 44
melting moments 85

meringues 78
meringue-topped berry
    tartlets 116–117
mint
    blackcurrant fruit
        loaf 42
    chocolate peppermint
        slice 67
muffins
    blueberry muffins 62
    chocolate muffins 63
mushroom and thyme
    toasts 109

N

nuts
    carrot and Brazil nut
        cake 24–25
    rich fruit ring cake
        12–13
    see also almonds;
        hazelnuts; walnuts

O

oats, oatmeal
    blueberry cheesecake
        114–115
    cheese and watercress
        scones 98
    flapjacks with
        apricots 74
    oat biscuits 86
    oatmeal and raisin
        cookies 87
    spiced oatmeal parkin
        49
onions
    bacon and onion
        tart 102
    red onion pastries 99

oranges
    melting moments 85
    Spanish orange and
        almond cake 30–31

P

palmiers 75
pears
    pear and almond
        tart 113
    rich fruit ring cake
        12–13
potatoes: spicy potato
    and leek quiche 100–101
prunes: rich fruit ring
    cake 12–13

Q

quiche lorraine 103

R

raspberries
    hazelnut meringue
        cake 28–29
    Scotch pancakes 76–77
redcurrants: meringue-
    topped berry tartlets
    116–117
Richmond maids of
    honour 119
ricotta cheese
    carrot and Brazil nut
        cake 24–25
    iced fairy cakes 71
    mushroom and thyme
        toasts 109
rock cakes 7

S

salmon
    broccoli quiche with
        salmon 104–105
    scrambled eggs with
        smoked salmon 108
    souffléd salmon tartlets
        96–97
scones 58
    blackberry and lemon
        scones 59
    cheese and watercress
        scones 98
Scotch pancakes 76–77
scrambled eggs with
    smoked salmon 108
seed cake 15
shortbread 83
Shrewsbury biscuits 91
shrimps: warm potted
    shrimps 107
Somerset apple cake 33
sour cream
    broccoli quiche with
        salmon 104–105
    honey cake 32
    quiche lorraine 103
Spanish orange and
    almond cake 30–31
strawberries
    meringue-topped berry
        tartlets 116–117
    strawberry shortcake
        34–35

T

teacakes 52
    cinnamon teacake 53
tomatoes: cheese and
    tomato rarebit 106
treacle tart 120–121

V
Victoria sandwich 20

W
walnuts
  coffee walnut cake 22
  date and walnut loaf 27
  rich fruit ring cake
    12–13
watercress: cheese and
  watercress scones 98

Teashop Treats Published in 2011 in the United Kingdom by
Vivat Direct Limited (t/a Reader's Digest),
157 Edgware Road, London W2 2HR

Teashop Treats is owned and under licence from The Reader's Digest Association, Inc.
All rights reserved.

We are committed both to the quality of our products and the service we provide our
customers. We value your comments, so please do contact us on **0871 351 1000** or
visit our website at www.readersdigest.co.uk. If you have any comments or suggestions
about the content of our books, email us at **gbeditorial@readerdigest.co.uk**

Illustrations: Anne Smith
Copy editor and additional text: Becky Alexander

For VIVAT DIRECT:
Editorial Director: Julian Browne
Art Director: Anne-Marie Bulat
Managing Editor: Nina Hathway
Trade Books Editor: Penny Craig
Prepress Technical Manager: Dean Russell
Production Controller: Jan Bucil

Colour origination by FMG
Printing and binding by Arvato Iberia, Portugal

ISBN 978-1-79020-041-5
Book code 400-546 UP0000-1